# TAKING ON STAFF

## Other How To Books on business and management

| | |
|---|---|
| Arranging Insurance | Master Book-Keeping |
| Be a Freelance Sales Agent | Master Public Speaking |
| Buy & Run a Shop | Organising Effective Training |
| Buy & Run a Small Hotel | Prepare a Business Plan |
| Collecting a Debt | Publish a Book |
| Communicate at Work | Publish a Newsletter |
| Conduct Staff Appraisals | Raise Business Finance |
| Conducting Effective Interviews | Selling Into Japan |
| Doing Business Abroad | Sell Your Business |
| Do Your Own Advertising | Start a Business from Home |
| Do Your Own PR | Starting to Manage |
| Employ & Manage Staff | Start Your Own Business |
| Investing in Stocks & Shares | Successful Mail Order Marketing |
| Keep Business Accounts | Taking on Staff |
| Manage a Sales Team | Understand Finance at Work |
| Manage an Office | Use the Internet |
| Managing Budgets & Cash Flows | Winning Presentations |
| Manage Computers at Work | Write a Report |
| Manage People at Work | Write Business Letters |
| Managing Meetings | Write & Sell Computer Software |
| Market Yourself | Your Own Business in Europe |

*Further titles in preparation*

The How To Series now contains more than 150 titles in the following categories:

Business Basics
Family Reference
Jobs & Careers
Living & Working Abroad
Student Handbooks
Successful Writing

Please send for a free copy of the latest catalogue for full details (see back cover for address).

BUSINESS BASICS

# TAKING ON STAFF

## How to recruit the right people for the job

**David Greenwood**

How To Books

Cartoons by Mike Flanagan

**British Library Cataloguing in Publication Data**

A catalogue record for this book is available from the British Library.

© Copyright 1996 by David Greenwood.

First published in 1996 by How To Books Ltd, Plymbridge House,
Estover Road, Plymouth PL6 7PZ, United Kingdom. Tel: Plymouth
(01752) 202301. Fax: (01752) 202331.

*Note:* The material contained in this book is set out in good faith for general
guidance and no liability can be accepted for loss or expense incurred as a
result of relying in particular circumstances on statements made in this book.
The laws and regulations may be complex and liable to change, and readers
should check the current position with the relevant authorities before making
personal arrangements.

Typeset by Concept Communications (Design & Print) Ltd, Crayford, Kent.
Printed and bound by The Cromwell Press, Broughton Gifford, Melksham,
Wiltshire

# Contents

# Contents

# List of Illustrations

# Preface

If your organisation is to develop and prosper in the twenty-first century you will need to take account of three things today.

1.  High levels of unemployment, allied to a variety of initiatives to equip people to make effective job applications, means that people who apply for jobs with your organisation probably have more experience in making good applications than you have in making the right recruitment decision.

2.  Vacancies which arise within your organisation will provide you with the best opportunities to realign and restructure in order to meet the challenges which you will face in an environment where 'change' is the only constant factor.

3.  Your ability to recruit the right people to the right jobs, and your ability to motivate and direct them towards your organisation's goals will be the keys to success.

In effect, your future depends on your skill in this area. This book offers an off-the-peg recruitment procedure appropriate to any organisation engaged in any kind of activity. It covers the entire process of recruitment and selection using checklists, questionnaires, specimen forms and contracts to put you in the driving seat ensuring that you will be prepared and able to act with speed and confidence when required to recruit, interview and select new staff.

It begins by questioning whether additional staff are really required and then it looks at the methods by which they may be found. At each stage in the process it suggests a variety of means by which evidence about a candidate's suitability for a job can be collected and assessed.

Finally, having laid the groundwork for the appointment of staff with premier league potential, it suggests ways in which your organisation can make the most of their skills, experience and potential so that your organisation achieves maximum benefit.

Throughout the book, the term 'he' is used rather than 'they' or the clumsier expression 'he/she'. Whilst the use of 'he' improves the readability of the text however, readers should be aware that it is used in this context to describe individuals of either gender and no sexism is intended.

*David Greenwood*

# 1
# Deciding the Job to be Done

Do you really need additional staff? Most hard-pressed managers would consider this to be an absurd question. It seems even more absurd if the apparent need is driven by the resignation or retirement of someone who has worked in a job for several years. 'Of course I need to replace him' is the obvious answer. 'Not next year or next month. I need a replacement today!'

At such times, it's hard to see beyond the immediate difficulties that a resignation can create. Maybe you do need to make a fast appointment, but before setting the recruitment process in motion, spend a short while looking at your current operation, the risks you face, and the range of opportunities available to you.

## LOOKING AT YOUR ORGANISATION

Most managers accept that **people** are their most important asset. They also acknowledge that problems with staff can give them their biggest headaches. Take two organisations with broadly similar products and the more successful will be the one with the better, more able and motivated staff. People can give your organisation the **competitive edge**. Recruiting the **right staff** can accelerate your organisation into the premier league. However recruitment can also be a double-edged sword. One poor appointment can drive your company into a steep and terminal nose-dive. In effect, people can make or break your company. **Recruitment is a high risk activity**.

### Assessing the risks
Some companies have very effective recruitment strategies. Others have none at all. Look at your business and think about the following:

1.  *Recruitment is a logical, step-by-step process which has a beginning, a middle and an end.* Recruiting staff can be less risky if you have a well planned system. Large organisations, for example, often

have personnel officers who are kept fully occupied, ensuring that there is a constant flow of well motivated, appropriately trained staff to fill vacancies as they arise. Smaller organisations, however, cannot afford such luxury. In your company the recruitment procedures, the standard forms and letters which large organisations use on a daily basis, may not exist at all. At a time when you need to act quickly, you may be unsure of how to proceed, ill-equipped to move the process forward, and required to *invent* your company's recruitment process – not just for this occasion by as a blueprint for the future.

2.   *Recruitment may be an obvious answer to your problem but it isn't necessarily the best solution.* When you are driven by an urgency to recruit, to 'fill the gap' in your organisation, there is a danger that you will be more aware of the problems arising from a failure to recruit, rather than the opportunities which can arise from resignations, retirements, or technological advances. The fear of how to get by without 'so-and-so', hides an important question: 'How should we make the best use of the opportunities that so-and-so's leaving has created?'

3.   *Recruiting the right staff requires careful preparation.* Many applicants for a job will be more experienced in the process than you. Many will have undergone several interviews already. They will have been taught about how to make good job applications and they will have had tuition in 'interview technique'. Lots of managers interview no more than two or three people in a given year. If recruitment is the solution to your problem, careful thought and preparation will be required.

## Considering employee characteristics

Bear in mind also that:

- staff are expensive

- unlike machines which behave in a reasonably predictable way, staff are a 'variable factor' in organisations – their quality can vary enormously

- employee potential can be difficult to assess

- staff can be easy to find, and hard to lose.

None of the above should put you off recruiting staff but it should encourage you to look carefully at your existing operation each time a vacancy arises and think about the size of the task facing you.

## CONSIDERING THE OPTIONS

A **vacancy**, no matter how it arises, provides you with an opportunity for development.

### Making the most of your opportunities
The need to recruit staff can be an opportunity to:

- redistribute the workload
- promote people within your organisation
- make savings
- update your operation
- change direction or emphasis.

### Identifying your options
Use a vacancy in your organisation to think about:

- *Restructuring.* Can the tasks which need doing be shared out and undertaken by existing staff?

- *Cancelling an aspect of your activity.* This may not be as silly as it sounds. Many companies are locked into history. They do things because they have always done them. Ask yourself: 'If I had to start again from a blank piece of paper, would I still want this done? If the answer is 'no', this may be your chance to update your operation. If the answer is 'yes', then ask yourself whether you would still want it done in the same way as it has been done in the past.

- *Contracting out aspects of your work.* Why not think about giving someone else the headache? Then all you need to do is keep an eye on the quality and the price.

- *Investing in new technology.* Computers don't moan or get tired. They don't demand overtime payments and they don't need holidays. In the early 1980s it was estimated that one word processor operator, working on a machine, considered primitive by today's standards, could cover the work of 17 typists. Since then, all types of business activities have been computerised. Upgrading your technology is always worth considering.

## MIXING AND MATCHING

Your organisation is unique and so it is unlikely that any of the above off-the-peg solutions will match your requirements perfectly. It's more likely that you'll use the opportunity to introduce a range of changes to improve your company's performance and potential. You may, for example, decide to cover the work of a retiring full-time member of staff by streamlining your operation, introducing new technology, promoting an existing member of staff, and advertising for a part-time assistant. In effect, although you may still choose to recruit someone, the job which you advertise may be very different to the job which was done by the member of staff who is leaving.

### Deciding what you need
Ask yourself:

● What is the cental purpose of my organisation?

● Are all tasks undertaken by my staff important to the cental purpose?

● Is my existing workforce fully occupied?

● Are my staff equipped to carry out their existing tasks efficiently?

● Are there people in my organisation who are ready to take on more responsibility?

● Do I have people who I want to reward?

● Is anyone in my organisation ready for promotion?

● Could aspects of my activity be carried out elsewhere, by machine, or by other people outside the organisation?

## DESCRIBING TASKS AND KEY AREAS OF WORK

Once you have established that recruitment is a valid part of your strategy for developing your organisation, and having got a general view of the type of work required, the next task is to begin describing the work you want done.

## Listing the tasks

Listing all the tasks within a job can be a useful starting point. If this job arises from the resignation or retirement of another employee, and if it remains largely unchanged, it can be useful to include that member of staff in this discussion. Presumably, he knows the job intimately and therefore he can help to ensure that nothing is overlooked.

Within a short time you will probably be able to produce a fairly long list of tasks which you need to be done by the new jobholder. They may not be in any logical order and, looking back at the list an hour or so later, you may discover that you have repeated yourself on a couple of occasions. If you have involved the current jobholder in this activity, you will probably also find that the list is highly detailed. Jobholders throughout an organisation always like to talk about the difficulty of their work and the level of responsibility it carries.

## Identifying the key areas

With a satisfactory list you can set about deleting repetition and grouping the tasks under a number of broad headings, ten at the most. These are the key areas of work which you want done. Figure 1 gives two examples of how tasks can be grouped together to identify key areas of responsibility.

## GETTING DOWN TO ESSENTIALS

Having identified the key areas, think generally about the skills, experience and knowledge someone would need in order to do this job well. Some skills will be *essential*. Without them, the job could not be done. Other skills will be *desirable*. These are the skills which would make life easier for both the jobholder and his manager.

## Determining the skills, experience and qualifications needed

The driver in the second example of Figure 1 would clearly need to be generally healthy and able to drive. A driving licence would be an essential qualification. You would probably also want to ensure that his licence was clean and that he had several years driving experience. For insurance reasons, you might also want to specify that candidates should be over a certain age and, because there is an element of vehicle

# Tasks and Key Areas

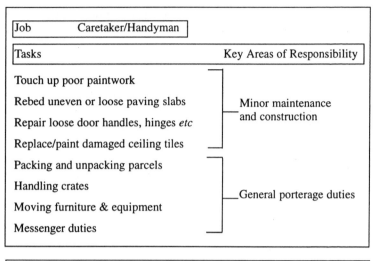

| Job | Caretaker/Handyman |
| --- | --- |

| Tasks | Key Areas of Responsibility |
| --- | --- |
| Touch up poor paintwork | |
| Rebed uneven or loose paving slabs | Minor maintenance and construction |
| Repair loose door handles, hinges *etc* | |
| Replace/paint damaged ceiling tiles | |
| Packing and unpacking parcels | |
| Handling crates | General porterage duties |
| Moving furniture & equipment | |
| Messenger duties | |

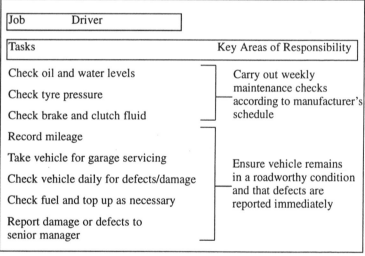

| Job | Driver |
| --- | --- |

| Tasks | Key Areas of Responsibility |
| --- | --- |
| Check oil and water levels | Carry out weekly maintenance checks according to manufacturer's schedule |
| Check tyre pressure | |
| Check brake and clutch fluid | |
| Record mileage | |
| Take vehicle for garage servicing | Ensure vehicle remains in a roadworthy condition and that defects are reported immediately |
| Check vehicle daily for defects/damage | |
| Check fuel and top up as necessary | |
| Report damage or defects to senior manager | |

Fig. 1. Example of how jobs can be grouped together to identify key areas of responsibility.

18

maintenance involved, you would probably also like candidates to have some knowledge of motor vehicle mechanics. This latter point may be *desirable* rather than *essential*.

## Thinking about experience

At this stage, try to keep a broad view of what you are looking for. Don't fall into the trap of being too specific about previous experience, or setting too much store by it. Experience can produce people with a depth of understanding and knowledge but:

● technical experience can become out of date very quickly

● in some cases five years experience of working in a job may be no better than two

● it can also produce cynical individuals, resistant to development and change

● it can teach people how to avoid any effort beyond the minimum required.

To be of any value to you, experience needs to have been good and relevant.

## Putting qualifications in perspective

Try to ensure also, that the qualifications you require are relevant and appropriate. It may be interesting, for example, to employ someone as a lifeguard who has a degree in archaeology, but a lifesaving certificate would be more relevant!

The qualifications necessary for some jobs are obvious, such as the driver and lifeguard mentioned above. Over recent years though, education has changed rapidly and currently there is a vast and confusing range of further education qualifications. Further details are given in the Appendix on page 137. For the moment however, think about whether you require someone who is qualified, or whether you are prepared to let experience make up for any lack of formal qualification. Consider also whether you are prepared to take on someone and offer appropriate on- and off-the-job training.

If you are looking for someone with a good level of general education you could simply state: 'A good general level of education is required.'

**Situations Vacant**

**Clerical Assistant**: duties include full office administration, all correspondence and maintaining of school accounts, including local management budget, monitoring and preparation of financial statements. Responsibility for arranging meetings, preparing agenda for governors' meetings, etc. Ability to drive school minibus and take after-school French Club an advantage. Salary £3,604 pa for 20 hours a week.

**Advertisement in Kent County Council internal newsletter.**
(Reported in *The Times Educational Supplement* 10/01/92)

Fig. 2. An advertisement for a school secretary.

### Setting out the lines of responsibility

Finally try to establish where this member of staff would be best located within your organisation. Who would they be responsible to? Lack of clarity on this point, even in the smallest of companies, can be disastrous. There are numerous horror stories concerning people appointed to work in small businesses and partnerships where the line of responsibility was never made clear. Usually, they jog along, managing to accommodate the wishes of the senior staff or owners, until the organisation comes under pressure or faces a crisis. At such times, the unfortunate member of staff may be pulled in every direction as each manager claims to have priority and asks for very different, often conflicting, tasks to be done immediately.

## REVIEWING YOUR DECISIONS

Armed with a general view of the nature of the job, the essential skills and knowledge required, and its location within your operation, take a few moments to ask yourself:

- Can this job really be done?

- Is the range of skills required too wide?

- Are the responsibilities appropriate?

- Is there likely to be anyone available with these qualifications?

- Is the job located correctly within the organisation?

Figure 2 is an advertisement for a school secretary published a few years ago. To the best of the author's knowledge there were no candidates.

## THINKING ABOUT TERMS

The size and nature of the job dictates, to a large extent, the **terms of employment** you will be able to offer. The options are quite extensive.

### Considering full-time and part-time options

The volume of work and the times of day when the work must be carried out are probably the factors which determine whether the job should be for a **full-time** position or for one or more **part-time** posts. Full-time jobs clearly remain popular among employees. Many employers also are happy to base their companies around a core of full-time staff who will remain with the organisation and develop skills appropriate to its needs. Employers in increasing numbers, however, are discovering advantages in employing staff on a part-time basis.

### Advantages in employing part-time staff

- Part-time staff can be employed to cover the peak times of day.

- They can increase the staff base, providing a pool of people who can be brought in to cover illness, peak periods in the yearly cycle, or annual holidays.

- They provide a pool of skilled labour who may be able to work extra hours if trade picks up.

- Part-time staff who work extra hours are often paid at their hourly rate whereas full-time staff could demand 'time and half' payments for overtime.

## Disadvantages in employing part-time staff

A part-time job may not attract as many candidates as a full-time post. Many people require full-time employment and will not respond to your vacancy. Of those who do, their desire for part-time work may imply that they have commitments elsewhere. The organisational flexibility which a large proportion of part-time staff seems to promise, may therefore be little more than an illusion.

Applicants seeking part-time work are often responding to short-term family commitments. When their situations change, you may not keep them for long.

Recruiting part-time staff can be as time-consuming as recruiting full-timers. You may need to go through the process more frequently and you'll need to exercise a great deal of care to ensure that you get 100 per cent commitment from them. Part-time work, after all, doesn't fill a person's life like a full-time job does.

## Employing permanent staff

Most managers readily accept that the old notion of a **permanent job**, a job for life, has disappeared for good. Today, permanent employment is achieved through an ability to move between a range of jobs, picking up a portfolio of useful skills and experience as you go. In this context though, *permanent* is used to describe work which is not carried out on short-term contract. The tasks you have listed, the skills required, the location of the job within the company, and the employment culture prevalent within the field of work, should provide you with the key to determining whether the job you have to offer should be permanent or short term. Work through the following checklist.

*Checklist*

- How close is this job to the central, core team of your organisation?

- Are the tasks 'ongoing', to be repeated regularly?

- Will there be a time, in the next eighteen months to two years, when they will have been achieved?

- Will technology overtake the need for this job in the foreseeable future?

- Is this vacancy the result of a temporary or permanent increase in activity?

- If the jobholder leaves the post after two years, will you need to replace him?

- Are staff with these skills easy to find?

- How much investment will you need to make in this person?

- Can you afford to let the benefit of that investment go to another company in the near future?

- Are short-term contracts an accepted employment practice in this particular area of work?

## Employing staff on short-term contracts

In general, the benefits of recruiting a keen, motivated, experienced and able member of staff on a permanent basis are well understood. **Short-term contracts**, however, can provide an interim solution at times of change. They can get you by until a permanent solution can be found. They allow you to hedge your bets. If activity doesn't pick up as you anticipate, the short-term contract will enable you to limit the damage to your company.

Bear in mind though, that a person who accepts a short-term contract may continue looking for a permanent job throughout his time with you. He may leave before the task has been completed and during his last six months his mind may be more attuned to securing other employment, than completing his contract.

## Using freelance staff

**Freelance staff** are self-employed specialists who undertake specific short-term tasks for companies. Many companies rely heavily on free-lancers. It is a way in which you can reduce in-house staff while calling upon the skills of a wide range of experts as and when you want them.

No business can afford to carry surplus staff these days, so in an ideal world the use of freelancers should enable you to increase or decrease your level of staffing to meet changes in demand for your services. Many companies buy in services and expertise, just as in the past they used to buy in components.

## Borrowing staff from elsewhere

If your need for a particular skill is short-term or highly specialist, why not consider **borrowing** a member of staff from a neighbouring organisation. Use your network and talk with colleagues and customers. It can be surprisingly easy to sell the idea, even to competitors, providing you can illustrate that it has attractions for all sides. You can often further your aims through co-operation rather than out-and-out competition. The 'Win Win' argument, with benefits to both organisation and the individual concerned, can be very powerful.

## DESCRIBING THE JOB

**Job descriptions** record the important facts about a job. They are essential documents which should be of benefit to both the organisation and the individual job holder by making simple, clear statements about what the job entails.

### Avoiding confusion

Much has been written about job descriptions and how they should be prepared. This is probably a reflection of their importance to employers, and the wide range of contexts in which they are used. A great deal of the available advice comes from personnel officers with background experience in large organisations. However, it doesn't always translate into the context of small and medium sized companies, so it is easy to be confused by the sometimes contradictory and inappropriate advice given.

Large organisations frequently produce several types of job description depending on the use to which the documents will be put. A job description prepared for consideration by a pay-board for example, will probably be a much more detailed and weightier document than one produced for recruitment purposes.

### Understanding the uses for job descriptions

As well as for recruitment purposes, a company may use **job descriptions** for:

- reviewing performance within a job
- establishing a suitable grade or rate of pay
- providing a basis for determining training needs
- judging the suitability of candidates.

Whenever dismissal has to be considered, or in cases which are referred to industrial tribunals, the job description is frequently used as a fundamental document in determining a course of action, or making a judgement.

So while managers in small companies often struggle to produce job descriptions which would stand the inappropriate scrutiny of a recruitment specialist from a large company, managers in larger organisations frequently sidestep their responsibilities by leaving this aspect of the recruitment process entirely to personnel staff. This is invariably a mistake. Many personnel officers are highly skilled in general recruitment but they are not technical specialists. In order to produce a comprehensive job description they need the in-depth knowledge of the job which only a manager can provide.

## Ensuring an appropriate job description

A good job description is a very powerful document. The most important thing about a job description however, is that it should work for you and your eventual member of staff. It it's done correctly, it will help you to:

- write the job advertisement
- produce a person specification
- shortlist
- prepare interview questions
- interview candidates
- check their abilities against your criteria
- identify their training needs
- support them in their efforts to fulfil the requirements of the post.

Essentially a job description is the basic document from which all else develops. If this sounds complicated or off-putting in any way, don't worry, you have already completed most of the work involved.

## PUTTING TOGETHER A JOB DESCRIPTION

Job descriptions should give the reader an understanding of the job by providing information such as:

- the job title
- the overall purpose of the job
- its location within the company
- reporting lines
- the key area of responsibility that the job carries.

Figure 3 provides the key headings which can be used as a basic format for a large number of jobs.

---

### Job Descriptions – The Key Headings

Most job descriptions can be written easily by using the following Key Headings:

1. **Job Title**
   Simply state the name of the job

2. **Reports to**
   On a day-to-day basis who is responsible for this person's work?

3. **Purpose of the Job**
   This should be a short one or two line statement. You may find it helpful to tackle this after you've completed the rest of the job description.

4. **Key Responsibilities**
   What is this person going to be responsible for? Try to list responsibilities rather than tasks.

5. **Knowledge and Experience Required**
   What knowledge, skill and experience is essential in order to carry out the job? What other attributes would be useful or desirable?

---

Fig. 3. Key headings for job descriptions.

## Determining the job title

Try to ensure that the title is a realistic description of the job and not simply a means of giving someone a grand title. Members of the public generally assume that people with similar titles carry similar responsibilities within a company so try to use the title to indicate the level of responsibility. For example, don't describe someone as a manager if they don't actually manage anyone.

## Locating the job within the organisation

Underneath the job title, make a simple statement about who the jobholder reports to. This locates the job within the organisation and gives readers a clear view of both the level of responsibility and seniority within the organisation. To avoid confusion at any later date, try to ensure that the reporting line is clean and uncluttered. Ideally, the jobholder should be responsible to one individual or body.

## Listing the key areas

Now list ten (or less) key areas of responsibility. Try to list them in order of priority, with the most important at the top. Begin each statement with an *action* verb – *produce, deliver, monitor, record, report, etc.*

If you feel further clarity is required, look again at the list of tasks you produced in order to identify those key areas of the job (refer to Figure 1 on p. 18 for illustration). Use one or two of the tasks to illustrate each key area.

## Deciding on the knowledge and experience required

A simple paragraph or two should be sufficient here. Prioritise your requirements by categorising knowledge and experience as *essential* or *desirable*.

## Setting the hours of work and conditions of service

This section should contain essential information regarding the nature of the job; full-time or part-time, temporary or permanent, shift arrangements, holidays, salary, and union agreements *etc.*

## Stating the overall purpose of the job

This paragraph should be placed above the list of key areas. For many people this can be the most difficult aspect of producing the job description so, for this reason, it often helps to approach this last. All that is required is a simple statement which describes the 'bottom line' of the job. Ask yourself this question: 'Stripped of all the frills, what is this job about?'

## Keeping it simple

Good job descriptions are those which can be read and understood with ease. Try to avoid over complicated words and concepts, repetition, and unnecessary verbage. Don't be afraid of brevity. The size and responsibility of a job is not related to the length or complexity of a job description. The vast majority of recruitment job descriptions can be written on one sheet of A4 paper. Lengthier ones invariably improve with editing. Make every word fight for its inclusion on the page.

The following job descriptions (Figures 4 and 5) illustrate how a variety of jobs can be described in simple terms.

## SUMMARY

● Before rushing to replace a member of staff, ask yourself whether recruitment is the best option. Recruitment may be an obvious answer to your problem but it isn't necessarily the *best* solution.

● People are an organisation's most important asset. They can also create the biggest headaches.

**Global Systems Ltd**
**Job Description**

**Job title**: Secretary

**Reports to**: Managing Director

### 1. Purpose of the job

To provide a full and confidential secretarial service for the Managing Director.

### 2. Key responsibilities

(a) Provide a full secretarial service, including word processing, audio and typing.

(b) Check all incoming mail, research background on routine items and either compose background notes or replies for signature by the Managing Director.

(c) Maintain a diary system and schedule appointments without reference to the Managing Director.

(d) Prepare agendas and take minutes at meetings.

(e) Act as the point of liaison between the Managing Director and senior managers, clients and the general public.

(f) Make travel arrangements for the Managing Director.

(g) Any other duties appropriate to the skills and experience of the job holder which may be identified by the Managing Director.

### 3. Knowledge and experience required

Excellent secretarial skills, a good command of the English language and very good organising skills are essential. The postholder must also be able to demonstrate an ability to deal efficiently with a wide cross-section of the public. Preference will be given to candidates who are familiar with a wide range of office software products and have a willingness to work as a member of a team in a small yet busy office.

Fig. 4. An example of a job description for a secretary.

**Victoria Ales**
**Job Description**

**Job title**:    Wages clerk

**Reports to**:   Finance Manager

### 1. Purpose of the job
To ensure that all staff receive an accurate, timely wage or salary payment and that the weekly and monthly payroll expenditure is correctly costed.

### 2. Key responsibilities
  (a)  Check timesheets for accuracy, query hours and overtime claimed if other than specified in contract.

  (b)  Input timesheet information into the computer and set up social security, income tax contributions.

  (c)  Ensure all payroll expenditure is accounted for and accurately costed to departments.

  (d)  Assist in the distribution of wages and salary slips.

  (e)  Prepare returns as necessary for tax and social security departments.

  (f)  Answer enquiries regarding wages scales, shift pay, service supplements, holiday entitlements etc.

  (g)  Maintain sickness and absentee records for all employees, ensuring that the appropriate deductions are made from wages and salaries.

  (h)  Other duties which may be assigned by the Finance Manager.

### 3. Knowledge and experience required
The postholder should have at least two years experience in a financial environment. Preference will be given to individuals with a general knowledge of wages and salary systems, social security and tax. The postholder should be able to communicate effectively at all levels. An understanding of computerised accounting/payroll systems would be an advantage.

Fig. 5. An example of a job description for a wages clerk.

- Recruiting staff can be less risky if you have a well planned system.

- Recruiting the right staff requires careful preparation.

- A vacancy, no matter how it arises, provides you with an opportunity for development.

- Your organisation is unique and so it is unlikely that any off-the-peg solutions will match your requirements perfectly.

- When you have a general view of the job, the essential skills and knowledge required, and its location within your operation, ask yourself whether this job can be done.

- Job descriptions record the important facts about a job. They are essential documents which benefit both the organisation and the individual.

- Try to avoid over complicated words and concepts in a job description. Make every word fight for its inclusion on the page.

## CASE STUDIES

### John's enthusiasm clouds the issues

John quickly convinces himself that recruitment is the right course of action for his organisation and that a new job description should be prepared. He wants to recruit the best possible candidate and so he spends a great deal of time trying to describe the job and the way it should be done. He consults with other staff and makes lengthy notes about the complexity of the job and the subtle qualities which will be required of someone to succeed in that post. The job description he produces covers three sides of A4 paper but it says little about the job which needs to be done. Somehow, John has been sidetracked into writing about *how* the job should be done and the *type* of person required. Key tasks are described at length but to the reader they seem more like key difficulties. The job description is difficult to use as a basis for a strategy for advertising or recruitment. To the reader, it seems more like an indictment of the organisation's lack of clarity and vision than a job description. As a result, other staff have to go through the same thought processes as John in order to gain a clear view of what they are looking for and how to succeed in the recruitment process.

## Trish pulls out the old job description

Trish is also convinced of the need to recruit quickly. In her view, if someone is leaving the organisation, she needs a replacement quickly. She feels fortunate that there is already an old job description for this post, and it should be relatively easy to use it as a basis for the new one. As the vacancy is for a secretarial position she asks a junior member of staff to look at the old job description and update it as necessary.

Although her member of staff is aware enough to change 'typing skills' to 'ability to use a word-processor', he fails to remove the need for someone 'able to take shorthand'. He also fails to appreciate that since the appointment of the last secretary to this post, the job has developed in several ways. There is now an electronic filing and scheduling system and it is now usual for the job holder to take minutes and prepare action sheets for senior managers at progress meetings. Trish's delegation and lack of attention to detail at this stage results in a crop of candidates without the required skill or experience.

## Mark puts the time in

Mark is a great believer in delegation. He appoints staff and expects them to grow into the job at speed. He prefers staff to take responsibility for their actions and generally to take appropriate decisions without constant need for referral or consultation. However, in order to achieve this he recognises the importance of recruiting the right people, and so he is unwilling to delegate the task of writing the job description to anyone else. This need to recruit staff has come at a difficult time but getting the recruitment process right is a priority for Mark if he wishes to fulfil his plans for the company. He burns the midnight oil in producing the job description and then runs it past his personnel people to 'dot the i's and cross the t's.' His investment of time at this stage, establishes a sound base for his recruitment strategy,

## DISCUSSION POINTS

1.  Do you really need a new member of staff?

2.  Does this vacancy give you an opportunity to reward any of your existing staff or restructure your organisation?

3.  Who is the most appropriate person in your organisation to write the job description?

# 2
# Setting up the Process

## TAKING AN OVERALL VIEW

Having described the job, the next task is to describe the person who you feel would be most able to fulfil all your requirements. This is usually done by writing a **person specification**. Various strategies are employed in producing this, but whichever system you choose it is important to avoid prejudice and to remain within the law.

### Using equal opportunities to advantage

The term equal opportunity defines the need to treat all people equally and fairly and without discrimination. Equal opportunity employers make particular efforts to ensure that they appoint the best person they can find for the job, irrespective of ethnic background, religious belief, gender or disability. Many employers support equal opportunities for the following reasons:

● They believe that it is right to do so.

● They feel that it is wrong to make assumptions about candidates simply on the strength of a little knowledge about gender, age or the colour of their skin.

● An employer needs the best staff he can possibly attract. He doesn't do himself any favours by ignoring applications on the grounds of irrational prejudice.

### Avoiding costly mistakes

Imagine that an employer could decide not to consider any woman for a post in an organisation. In effect the employer will have chosen to make a selection from only a half of the potential population. How can he be sure that the ideal candidate for this job lies in the half of the population he is prepared to consider?

## Staying within the law

Equal opportunities is an umbrella term for a number of Acts of Parliament. There is no single equal opportunity law and there is nothing in the law which states that you must be an equal opportunity employer. All companies however, must as a minimum, fulfil the requirements of a number of laws which make employment discrimination against certain groups illegal.

- **The Equal Pay Act 1970** (amended in 1983) stipulates that an employee is entitled to equal pay (and other contractual terms and conditions) with an employee of the opposite sex if they are doing work which is the same or broadly similar, or if the work they do has been rated as equivalent by job evaluation or in terms of the demands made on the worker.

- **The Sex Discrimination Acts of 1975 and 1986** make it unlawful to discriminate:
  - in the arrangements made for deciding who is offered a job;
  - in the terms on which the job is offered;
  - in deciding who is offered the job;
  - in making opportunities available for promotion, transfer or training:
  - in the benefits, facilities, or services granted to employees;
  - in dismissals, or other unfavourable treatment of employees.

- **The Race Relations Act 1976** makes it unlawful to discriminate against anyone because of race, colour, nationality, ethnic or national origins. The Act applies to jobs and training as well as housing and education.

- **The Disabled Persons (Employment) Acts of 1944 and 1958** require employers, with more than 20 staff, to employ a quota of registered disabled people. The current quota is 3 per cent. In 1992, only 20 per cent of companies met their quota. Only ten prosecutions have ever been brought for failure to comply with the requirements of this law and no company has been prosecuted since 1975. The government argues that with only 1 per cent of the workforce registered as disabled, companies cannot possibly meet their quota and therefore it would be unfair to prosecute them. Why do so many disabled people choose not to register their disability? There are probably a number of reasons for this. Undoubtedly though, many feel that they have a better chance of gaining employment by not drawing attention to their disability.

## DESCRIBING THE PERSON

Just as a **job description** describes a job, so a **person specification** describes the person most suitable to do it. Many managers find the easiest way to do this, is to write brief paragraphs about their ideal candidate under five or six general headings. Some managers like to use a five-point plan.

### Using the five-point plan
You can use the **five-point plan** headings to describe your ideal candidate.

- Qualifications, knowledge appropriate to the job.
- Specific skills, abilities and aptitudes required.
- Experience required.
- Personal attributes.
- Physical attributes.

### Determining the qualifications
Deciding what qualifications you will require your ideal candidate to have can be a major headache. There are three problems.

1.  At the moment there is a confusing array of school, further education and higher education qualifications. Many of them are described by the name of the examining board such as City and Guilds, BTec, and RSA. This tells you something about the organisation which set the examination and marked the work but nothing about the level of skill or knowledge which was required by the candidate who holds the certificate.

2.  Adult job hunters may have qualifications which are now obsolete. Only you can decide whether a qualification in, for example typing, will be of any use in an office which consigned its typewriters to the scrapheap a few years ago in favour of word processors.

3.  It is easy to be seduced by qualifications. People use them like medals or decorations. When you decide what qualifications are needed, try to describe the *minimum* qualification required and

make sure it is relevant to the job. Is a PhD in food technology an essential requirement for a confectionary sales manager? Is a grade C GCSE in maths essential for someone working at a checkout in a supermarket?

## Comparing qualifications

Thanks to the introduction of **National Vocational Qualifications (NVQs)**, it is becoming easier to describe the type and level of qualifications you require. Essentially NVQs recognise and give credit for workplace skills. They are awarded at different levels to reflect the degree of skill required in different types of job. NVQ level *two* is regarded as roughly the equivalent of four good GCSEs; NVQ level *three* carries the same weight as two A levels; and NVQ level *four* is considered to be equivalent to a first year university level of study. Currently there are NVQ qualifications covering 86 per cent of jobs and more are being developed all the time. Figure 6 is a chart which lists the more popular qualifications and places them appropriately on the NVQ four-rung ladder.

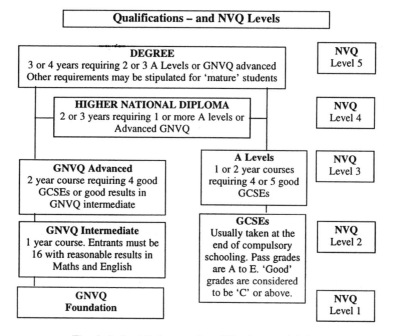

Fig. 6. A chart listing usual qualifications and their
relationship to the NVQ levels.

## Avoiding problems with qualifications

If you are unsure about existing qualifications when writing a person specification, you can avoid problems by listing areas of knowledge which you require, rather than specific examinations passed. A boat-builder for example may need knowledge of glass fibre laminating and lay-up techniques, a shipping clerk may need to be familiar with export procedures, a book-keeper may need to know about double-entry systems. Some occupations have fairly standard qualifications which are known and accepted throughout the UK. In such cases, it is enough to stipulate that you need 'qualified' staff. In this way, having stated that you require qualifications, the onus is then on the candidate to prove that the certificates he holds are relevant to the job and of the right level. The Appendix (page 137) contains brief descriptions of some of the types of qualifications you may find mentioned in job applications.

## Describing specific skills, abilities and aptitudes

In this part of the **person specification** think about the skills someone would need in order to be successful in the job. A candidate for a management post may need to be able to negotiate with trade unions, another manager may need to have the ability to close deals and contracts. A journalist needs to have interviewing and networking skills and the ability to grasp complex issues and present then in a form which can be understood by ordinary members of the public. Some jobs require a high level of problem-solving skills. Others require an ability to work to high levels of precision. Some jobs may require manual skill and dexterity.

**Aptitude** is often used to describe a feeling for the essential characteristics of a job. An aptitude for using numbers or words for example.

## Determining the experience required

What sort of experience does the job require? Some jobs require no experience at all. Others need qualified staff and this frequently means that they have served their time as apprentices or trainees. Some jobs carry supervisory responsibilities, in which case you would be looking for someone who has obtained the basic qualifications and then had a few years good experience in the business. However, don't fall into the trap of measuring experience simply by time spent in a company or in an activity. For higher-level management jobs, for example, you might be looking for someone with breadth, *as well* as length of experience; someone who has worked in a number of organisations and who has picked up a portfolio of good practice from a variety of sources.

Remember too that *experience* can be a double-edged sword. You're looking for *good* experience.

## Describing the personal attributes you require

Some jobs are highly repetitive and need patience and persistence. Others require people to cope with high levels of stress. Some demand tough-minded characters, whereas other jobs are better suited to people who listen and analyse situations sympathetically. Think about the job and the environment in which it is to be carried out. What type of person would perform best? Bear in mind that some attributes aren't necessarily attractive qualities in people. The nature of the job may demand a level of ruthlessness, abrasiveness, or a willingness to take risks.

## Taking account of the physical attributes

A minority of jobs require high levels of physical strength and ability. Likewise, some jobs are only suitable for the able-bodied. Many however, have no such requirement. One of the most common reasons given by employers for not employing disabled people is that they have no suitable jobs.

*Weighing up the evidence*

- A recent survey of employers in Sussex found that 41 per cent of employers thought that their field of work was unsuitable for disabled people. Other employers in the same occupational areas however, thought that disabled people would be suitable. Clearly, there are some myths and prejudices about disability.

- Some myths suggest that disabled people are less productive and have poor sickness records. This is not true. In 1948 the US government carried out a survey of work records of 48,000 disabled people. The researchers came to the conclusion that there was no difference in productivity, absenteeism, or safety records between disabled and able-bodied workers.

- Employers who have given disabled people a chance seem to be pleased with the results. A survey in Devon showed that 93 per cent of employers who had disabled people in their workforce found them to perform as well or better than able-bodied workers; 43 per cent reported that their attitude to work was better and 70 per cent felt that disabled workers' attendance was good. 26 per cent of employers thought it was better.

**Global Systems Ltd**
**Secretary to the Managing Director**
**Person Specification**

**Physical attributes**

General good health. Clean businesslike presentable appearance. Articulate.

**Attainments**

Good general level of education with GCSE grade 'C' or equivalent in English and Mathematics. Competence in use of a wide range of PC software packages supported by experience or FE qualifications in Office Practice. Experience of work establishing and maintaining office systems, dealing with the public, scheduling meetings, taking minutes and preparing agendas.

**Intelligence**

An ability to think logically and sequentially. An eye for detail and an ability to establish effective plans and schedules. An alert mind.

**Special aptitudes**

A self-motivated person who is able to set priorities and goals. A team worker, with high level of 'people skills' in dealing with managers, staff, clients and members of the public.

**Interests**

An interest in current affairs and an interest in people would be of benefit to the postholder in his or her work.

**Disposition**

An outgoing yet discreet and dependable person with a care and interest in people. An ability to cope with the stress and pressure of a busy office in a highly competitive business. A teamworker, assertive rather than aggressive when required.

**Circumstances**

The postholder must be prepared to travel within the UK at times. This is an occasional rather than regular requirement.

Fig. 7. A completed person specification using the seven-point plan.

The main problem seems to be that employers are unaware of how *able* a *disabled* person can be. As a result they assume that the jobs they have to offer would only suit an able-bodied person. Take care. You could fail to attract some excellent candidates if you wrongly assume that the job you have to offer could not be done by a disabled person.

## Using more sophisticated systems

A more detailed person specification can be developed using a seven-point plan developed by Professor A. Roger at the National Institute of Industrial Psychology.

*The seven-point plan*

1. *Physical attributes*  health, physique, appearance, bearing, speech

2. *Attainments*  academic qualifications, training received, experience and skills, acquired knowledge

3. *Intelligence*  general intelligence, specific abilities

4. *Special aptitudes*  mechanical, manual, verbal, numerical, artistic

5. *Interests*  personal interests as possible indicators of aptitudes, abilities or personality traits such as practical, constructional, intellectual, social

6. *Disposition*  equability, dependability, self-reliance, assertiveness, drive, energy, perseverance, initiative, motivation

7. *Circumstances*  personal and domestic circumstances, mobility, commitments, social/cultural background

## USING YOUR PERSON SPECIFICATION

Figure 7 is a completed person specification using the seven-point plan. Person specifications can be used in a number of ways. Initially, they help in the writing of a job advertisement. Later you can use them as tools to help you to produce a shortlist of candidates from a large number of applications. Your person specification, for example, may require the successful candidate to hold a clean driving licence. Therefore, you can automatically discount any applicant who doesn't meet this requirement. It may also demand proven ability in maths, or experience of handling people in difficult situations. Once again, without evidence of either of these, you can filter out more applicants until you arrive at a small group of people who appear to fit the bill.

Equal opportunity employers often take the process a stage further by using the person specification as a checklist to record how they arrive at the decision to employ a particular person in favour of the four or five other shortlisted candidates. Testing candidates against the requirements of a well-written person specification allows an employer to prove that the decision not to employ someone was based on a requirement of the job rather than discrimination against ethnic background, religion, or disability.

## LOOKING AT THE OPTIONS

With a well prepared job description and person specification you have arrived at a milestone in the recruitment process. You know what you want done and you have a view about the ideal person to do it for you. At this stage there are two options available to you. You could:

- hand over the process to a commercial recruitment agency
- continue the recruitment process yourself.

Commercial recruitment agencies frequently offer a **complete recruitment package** and it is quite possible to involve them in the recruitment process well before this stage. Their effectiveness however is dependent upon their ability to gain answers to three questions:

- What job do you want done?
- What is your company like?
- What sort of person would be best able to meet your requirements?

Clearly, you are the best able to answer these questions and so earlier contact with commercial agencies would only result in them holding discussions with you in order to produce a job description and person specification. In effect, you would still be required to describe the job and the ideal candidate.

## USING RECRUITMENT AGENCIES

**Recruitment agencies** will find staff for a fee. You can use the expertise of their professional interviewers rather than spend too much time working through the process yourself. A good recruitment agency will try to get to know your company well. Its staff will try to ensure that they know your product or service, the working atmosphere, the benefits, the number of people you employ, and your priorities. They should know the qualities each company is looking for in its staff and the level of speed, accuracy and skill required. They take time and trouble to find suitable people to fill vacancies as they arise. Their credibility is based upon their ability to provide suitable recruits who can fill vacancies with a minimum of fuss and disruption.

You can use recruitment agencies to advertise your vacancy and interview candidates on your behalf. Interviewers are usually highly trained, experienced professionals so you can expect them to do a thorough job for you. Most recruitment agencies are very discreet and they are extremely careful not to disclose confidential information to other clients. Many agencies specialise in recruiting staff to particular areas of work so they can be very useful in cases where you wish to recruit someone with fairly general knowledge of a certain kind of work: a secretary, or an accountant for example. There are specialist recruitment agencies for most areas of work. You'll find them listed in *Yellow Pages*.

### Considering the pros and cons

As in all things, there are advantages and disadvantages in handing over the process to other people:

*Pros*
- Professional recruiters are usually highly trained and experienced.

- Private recruitment agencies depend on meeting your requirements in order to stay in business.

- Handing over the recruitment process will allow you to concentrate on keeping your business running.

- Many agencies may already know of suitably qualified and experienced people able to fill your vacancy immediately.

*Cons*
● Agencies charge fees.

● No recruitment agency can know your business as well as you.

● How much importance do you place on selecting the right person
  for this job? If it's important, can you really afford to delegate the
  responsibility to someone else?

## OPTING FOR DIY RECRUITMENT

Recruitment agencies can be particularly effective when it comes to
recruiting people on a short-term basis. A temp secretary or seasonal
staff for a restaurant or a bar for example. When it comes to recruiting
staff who will be part of the permanent *core* team within your organisation, there is much to be recommended in doing it yourself. If this
sounds like a daunting prospect, think about the damage which could be
caused by recruiting the wrong person. Anyway relax, you've done the
hard slog, you're over half-way through the process and the rest of the
work is much more fun!

### Taking the first steps

DIY recruitment is a logical and sequential activity. It is a process of
small steps which lead towards the recruitment of a member of staff who
will fulfil all the requirements of the post, bringing the necessary skills
and attitudes with them. It doesn't happen by accident. It happens
because you take the time and trouble to make sure it happens. You now
know what you want done and you know the sort of person you want to
do it for you. The next step is to decide how to collect the evidence
which will enable you to spot the most likely candidates.

### Deciding what you need to know

To begin with, it is important to establish a means of deciding whether
an applicant has the right mix of skills, qualifications, experience, background and temperament *etc*. Does this sound familiar to you? It should
do, we're talking here about the job description and the person specification which you have written. In general, there are two options available. You can ask candidates to write a **letter of application** or you can
ask them to complete an **application form**.

*Asking for letters of application*
Many employers advertise for staff, asking enquirers to 'apply in writing

to . . .'. With this strategy you take the risk and hope that the letters you receive will contain enough information for you to get an accurate view of each applicant's suitability. Unfortunately, whilst this method allows you to draw some conclusions, they are usually negative ones. It's easy, for example, to discard the untidy, poorly or hastily written letter in favour of the better presented application. Without asking for a particular framework of information however, both letters could be omitting vital information which, if known, could possibly reverse the decision you made.

Letters of application also make it difficult to compare the apparent strengths and weaknesses of different candidates. Each letter of application will be very different, laying emphasis on some aspects of the job and skirting over, or possibly ignoring, other topics. In effect, letters of application make it very difficult to compare like with like among applicants.

*Using application forms*
With an application form you take control of your information needs. Application forms put you in the driving seat. They make applicants give you the information you require rather than the information they choose to let you have.

## CREATING APPLICATION FORMS

If your company doesn't have a standard job application form, your local Jobcentre can supply a general form which you can use. It is far better however, to spend time putting one together for yourself. A good application form can be used for a large number of jobs and so the effort of creating a good one is worthwhile. Organisations' application forms can look wildly different, largely because of layout. In truth though there are probably more similarities than differences. Most ask for very similar details such as:

- applicant's name
- address
- telephone number – home and work
- age and date of birth
- sex
- nationality
- education and training
- health

- employment history
- hobbies and interests
- names and addresses of referees.

Most forms also have a section headed 'additional information' or 'further information' which enables a candidate to give additional information in support of his application.

### Establishing a layout

It makes a great deal of sense to locate basic information requirements such as name, age, address *etc* on the front page of your application form. This puts the applicant in the frame and allows you to contact him easily. Questions about age and marital status are also frequent front-page items so that it is easy for you to photocopy the front page of the successful candidate's form and send it on to the wages and pensions department if you have one. Everything they need to know about the candidate is contained on that single piece of paper so it is easy to assimilate the new member of staff onto the payroll with a minimum of fuss. Likewise, a copy of the front page is also a good starting point for the establishment of an **employee record file**.

Figures 8 and 9 show examples of two different application forms. It should be easy to use either as a basis for producing your own. Many computer software systems are capable of producing simple forms such as these. For a professional looking job for your company, you could try approaching one or two printing companies listed in *Yellow Pages*.

*Testing the form*

Before investing in a large-scale print run however, ask a couple of colleagues to try to complete the form you have designed. This should enable you to discover whether the questions are clear and whether you have left sufficient room on the form for the applicant's answers. It can also be useful to have a friend from outside the company cast his eye over it. What impression does the form make on him?

- Is it neat?
- Is it well layed out?
- Is your company logo or trademark clearly identifiable?
- Is it easy to complete?
- Does it tell an applicant where to return the form?

*Proofreading*
Finally, double check the spelling of each and every word. Remember, many job applicants will also be customers. Your application form will tell an applicant a great deal about the standards you set for your operation.

## GETTING ADDITIONAL HELP

Government employment services can help you at various stages in your recruitment process. The initial point of contact is your local **Jobcentre**. As with most government initiatives, the level and style of help can change from time to time. In general however, Jobcentres offer the following services to employers:

● **Advice** on your recruitment methods and procedures.

● **Information** about the availability of suitable candidates and the local labour market.

● **Interview facilities** at some Jobcentres.

● **Distribution of application forms** – yours or theirs.

● **Access** to information and advice about a variety of employment and training issues.

    In effect, you can use the Jobcentre to:

● **Circulate your vacancy** – locally or nationally by computer and on teletext.

● **Provide help with interviews** – tell them how many people you want to interview and they won't refer more than this number to you. You can hold your interviews at the Jobcentre if you wish.

● **Send you suitable applicants** – you can discuss and agree needs with Jobcentre staff. Give them a list of essential requirements and they'll do the initial screening.

*Enhanced services*
These are available if you require extra help.

**Arts and Crafts Ltd**

Please return this form to the Managing Director – Arts & Crafts Ltd 12–15 Grouville Way, Castleford, West Yorkshire.

## Application for employment

*Please use ink and CAPITAL letters when you fill in this form*  For Official Use Only

| Post applied for | | Date received |
|---|---|---|

### Personal Details

Title   | Mr | Mrs | Miss | Ms |

*(tick as appropriate)*

Daytime telephone number

First Names

Evening telephone number

Surname

Address

Date of birth

The educational Qualifications you have obtained

Apprenticeships or traineeships you have completed

Recent courses you have attended

Other skills relevant to this job

Previous employment

| Name of employer | From | To | Brief details of duties | Reasons for leaving |
|---|---|---|---|---|
| | | | | |

Fig. 8. An example of an application form layout.

46

Health        Does your health stop you from doing certain types of work?

| Yes | | No | | (tick as appropriate) |

If yes – please give details

Hobbies & Interests

Referees

Please give the names and addresses of two persons, not related to you, from whom references may be obtained. You should obtain their permission before returning this form.

Name..........................................    Name..........................................

Business or Occupation ..............    Business or occupation...............

Address ......................................    Address ......................................

..................................................    ..................................................

..................................................    ..................................................

..................................................    ..................................................

Telephone number.......................    Telephone number ......................

Further Information

State any other details in support of your application

I confirm that the information given in this application is complete and correct

Signed

Date

Fig. 8. continued.

# CENTREFORCE SYSTEMS Ltd
## APPLICATION FORM

### TECHNICAL SECRETARIAL & SUPPORT STAFF

PLEASE USE BLOCK CAPITALS

| | |
|---|---|
| Position applied for | For official use only |
| First names | Date received |
| Surname | Date acknowledged |
| Address | Telephone |
| | Date of birth |
| | Do you have a clean driving licence? |
| | *Please tick* Yes No |

Previous employment

| Name of employer | From | To | Details of job | Reason for leaving |
|---|---|---|---|---|
| | | | | |

Fig. 9. An example of a different application form layout.

## Education

Please give details of schools and colleges attended, and qualifications obtained

| School | From | To | Qualifications obtained |
|--------|------|-----|-------------------------|
|        |      |     | *Please use a continuation sheet if necessary* |

## Training

Please list recent training courses attended

| Course | Date | Location |
|--------|------|----------|
|        |      | *Please use a continuation sheet if necessary* |

## Referees

Please give the names and addresses of two people from whom references may be obtained

Name

Occupation

Address & Telephone

Name

Occupation

Address & Telephone

I confirm that the information given in this application is complete and correct

Signed                          Date

*Please return to centreforce systems Ltd Century House Woodford Leeds KL6 7TF.*

Fig. 9. continued.

49

- **Job interview guarantees** – offer extra help in selecting people to fill your vacancies.

- **Job preparation courses** – prepare jobseekers for interview.

- **Work trials** – allow you to assess, at no cost, how an applicant performs in the job.

*Points to remember*
Bear in mind however, that Jobcentres are primarily in the business of getting people back to work and they are highly successful at doing this. There are 1,079 Jobcentres in the UK and in 1993–94 they handled 2,180,192 vacancies. During the same period they placed 1,791,982 people in employment. Your aims are different. You aren't necessarily looking to reduce the number of unemployed people. Your job is simply to find the most appropriate candidates for the job you have to offer. A working partnership with Jobcentre staff and services can be highly effective. After all, partnerships work best when different people combine their different strengths and talents. It's important though that you realise from the outset that you may both be working to slightly different agendas.

## SUMMARY

- You don't have to be an equal opportunity employer but you *must* comply with the requirements of the law.

- An employer who ignores applications on the grounds of irrational prejudice can do his company a great deal of harm.

- Just as a job description describes a job, so a person specification describes the person who would be best able to do it.

- When you decide on the qualifications required to do a job, try to describe the *minimum* qualifications required and make sure they are relevant to the job.

- If you are unsure about qualifications when writing a person specification, you can avoid problems by listing areas of knowledge which you require, rather than specific examinations passed.

- Don't measure experience simply by time spent in a company or in an activity. Remember you're looking for *good* experience.

- A person specification can be used in a number of ways. Initially, it helps in the writing of a job advertisement. Later you can use it as a tool to help you to produce a shortlist of candidates from a large number of applications.

- Having written a job description and a person specification there are three options open to you. You can hand over the process to a commercial recruitment agency, allow a government agency to identify appropriate candidates for you, or continue the recruitment process yourself.

- When recruiting staff who will be part of the permanent *core* team within your organisation, there is much to recommend seeing the process through from beginning to end.

- Letters of application allow candidates to decide what information *they* will give *you*.

- With an application form you take control of your information needs. Application forms put you in the driving seat. They make applicants give you the information you require.

- Check your application form carefully before sending it to the printer, it tells an applicant a great deal about the standards you set for your operation.

- You can obtain additional help and advice from your local Jobcentre.

## CASE STUDIES

### John closes down his options

In describing the best person for the job, John finds himself in a discussion with Jobcentre staff who ask whether he might be prepared to consider a disabled person. John dismisses the idea without much thought. The office is located on the first floor which can only be accessed by a stairway. 'No one in a wheelchair would ever get up there,' he reasons. It doesn't occur to him that not all disabled people are wheelchair bound.

## Trish looks in the mirror

Having decided to take some time over producing a person specification, Trish thinks about the *type* of person she would like to have around her in the workplace. Her thoughts centre mainly on the personality attributes which would lend themselves to an easy relationship between her and her new member of staff. Phrases such as 'pleasant personality', 'well mannered and friendly' are to be found throughout the person specification which she writes. A colleague sums up the problems with her person specification by commenting that Trish's requirements read as if she is looking to recruit a 'clone'. 'Were you thinking about the job or staring into the mirror when you wrote this?' he asks.

## Mark works out his priorities

Mark decides that he needs to invest a substantial amount of time in getting the person specification right. Clearly he needs someone who he will be able to work with but he realises also, that the strength of an organisation can often rely upon the differences between people and the wealth of knowledge and experience they bring with them. Deciding the right mix of experience, knowledge and personal attributes therefore, is a crucial requirement of the recruitment process. He's already invested a great amount of time on this vacancy however, and so he needs to find a way of speeding up the process. Fortunately he discovers that the application form published by the Jobcentre is almost perfect for his needs. He can afford to devote more time to producing the person specification because he knows that, thanks to the Jobcentre, he can move through the next part of the process fairly quickly.

## DISCUSSION POINTS

1.  With a job description and a person specification do you feel you have enough information to know what you are looking for?

2.  Are you comfortable with handing over the recruitment process to professional agencies or would you prefer to see the process through yourself?

3.  Have you made a point of keeping the door open for potentially good candidates by ensuring that misconceptions about age, ability or gender haven't clouded your thinking?

# 3
# Trawling the Field

## ADVERTISING FOR STAFF

Some companies rarely need to advertise for staff. Their reputation as good employers or leaders in the field is enough to ensure that they have a constant stream of enquiries from would-be employees. Many small neighbourhood businesses also receive numerous speculative enquiries from friends, school-leavers and customers. It is worthwhile keeping a file of names and addresses and it would do no harm to trawl through them before committing yourself to needless effort and expense. Often though, the 'speculative enquiries' file offers only a partial solution. Information such as this becomes obsolete very quickly. The school-leaver or college graduate who contacted you in June may have moved on by September. He could be trekking round the world by now. The young mother who was seeking a part-time book-keeping job last week may have solved her child-minding problems so now she could be looking for full-time rather than part-time work. In truth, most companies looking for staff need to let people know that a vacancy exists and there are a number of advertising options available.

### Using word-of-mouth recruitment methods

If your organisation is highly specialised, you may already know the local key players and where the talent lies. In such cases, advertising your vacancy may require little more than a well placed remark to colleagues over lunch or during a telephone conversation. Then you can let the network do the rest.

**Word-of-mouth** advertising works well if you are sure that:

- your message will reach the right people
- there are strong candidates to be found locally
- you can attract the right person from a relatively narrow field.

However, word-of-mouth advertising is rarely a complete solution, because it is unlikely that all your potential candidates will get to hear of the vacancy within the timescale you set – and they may not hear of it at all. So by restricting your advertising, you aren't opening the door as wide as you should. The best candidate could slip through your fingers because he didn't know you wanted him. It fails completely if you are unsure of the local scene.

Some employers resort to asking staff if they have friends who might like a job. This is always a dangerous strategy. All too often, names are suggested on the basis of friendship rather than the ability to do a job, and rejection of such candidates usually demotivates the staff who made the suggestion.

## Using display cards

**Display cards** placed in shop windows, on boards in supermarkets, or within public areas of your own premises can be effective. It's an inexpensive option which works well if you are looking to recruit:

- unskilled staff
- local people with fairly general skills
- part-time staff
- women returners
- customers who could becomes employees.

Unfortunately this strategy relies upon your ideal recruit walking past the right window and taking time to study it. It is also limited by the profile of readership. Cards can be very effective in recruiting people who are seeking to return to work, but no use at all for attracting skilled staff already in employment. To have any effect at all, the placement of display cards must be carefully thought out.

## Recruiting through Jobcentre ads

Anyone who is unemployed and looking for a job, should visit the Jobcentre on a regular basis. Without a doubt, a display card there will be seen by a large number of people and many, with the help of Jobcentre staff, will be encouraged to apply for the post you advertise. Applications however, will need careful screening. Most people who visit Jobcentres are unemployed. They need a job *but not necessarily* the job you advertise – any job will do. People in employment, seeking to change their jobs, rarely visit Jobcentres. You'll probably get lots of enquiries but beware of those who make contact and say: 'The Jobcentre sent me!' Advertising your vacancy in the Jobcentre isn't a complete solution. You may find your ideal candidate there, but don't rely on it.

## Advertising in local newspapers

Most areas of the country have at least one regular local newspaper as well as a number of freesheets. Some areas also have regional papers published each evening which reach a wider readership. Local newspapers offer you the opportunity to:

- advertise your vacancy quickly
- reach a large number of local people
- target a particular geographical area.

## Choosing the right local newspaper

The most appropriate local paper depends upon the type of job you have to offer. An advertisement in the freesheet may be adequate for recruiting someone to an unskilled job, whereas if you are seeking someone with fairly general skills it may be better to advertise in the local newspaper. For more specific skills, you may need to cast your net wider and advertise in the regional paper. Try to imagine your ideal candidate and ask yourself which paper he is most likely to read.

- The freesheet may be cheaper but is it read by potential employees?

- Is the local evening paper better for your needs?

- Does your ideal candidate live around the corner or do you need to advertise further afield?

## Getting the facts

Editors take great trouble to stay in touch with their readership so, as a potential advertiser, a simple phone call to each paper should tell you:

- the size of readership
- the distribution area
- the readership profile
- the cost of advertising.

This should enable you to decide which newspaper is most likely to be read by people able to fill the position you have to offer but, before dashing to the phone, remember that this strategy also has a couple of weaknesses:

- your advertisement will be read by a large number of people who cannot fill your vacancy;
- today's newspaper is tomorrow's chip wrapper!

## Advertising in national newspapers

For professional or highly specialist staff an advertisement in a national newspaper may be more appropriate. It could still end its days as a fish and chip wrapper, having been read by a large number of disinterested people, but some editors have reduced these problems by running advertisements for particular types of job on different days of the week. *The Guardian* for example operates the following advertising schedule:

- Monday:     Creative occupations, media, marketing and secretarial work
- Tuesday:    Educational vacancies
- Wednesday:  Public appointments
- Thursday:   Commercial jobs
- Friday:     The environment and housing sectors

*The Times* schedule is:

- Monday:     Secretarial and education
- Tuesday:    Legal appointments
- Wednesday:  Media and marketing
- Thursday:   Public appointments, information technology, accounting and engineering posts

Other newspapers prefer to put all their job advertisements together on the same day. The *Daily Mail*, for example, publishes the bulk of theirs each Thursday.

As with local newspapers, it pays to obtain circulation details, profiles of readership and advertising rates before deciding where your advertisement would be best placed. Use the person specification you have prepared. Does your ideal candidate read *The Sun* or *The Guardian*?

## Magazine advertising

The large number of magazines you see on newsagents' shelves are just the tip of a huge iceberg. For every one displayed there are at least another three in circulation which you have probably never heard of. At the last count there were no less than 9,432 periodicals regularly published in the UK. Many are 'trade' publications written for those involved in specific business activities. There is a magazine for almost every kind of occupation from architects to zookeepers. You probably already know most of them related to your field of activity. Almost all carry advertisements enabling you to target a much more specific type of reader. Magazines tend to be kept longer than newspapers, and they are passed around much more. So, although sales are often less, readership can be greater. Lists of magazine titles and contact addresses are published in *Willings Press Guide*. It is available in most public libraries.

Magazine advertisements are effective in:

● recruiting enthusiasts who enjoy their work and enjoy reading about it

● reaching people with particular professional skills or interests

● spreading your net beyond local or regional boundaries.

Unfortunately magazines are not so good at meeting the needs of managers who are in a hurry. You cannot place an 'instant' advertisement in a monthly magazine.

Figure 10 suggests the most appropriate advertising for different types of staff. The most successful recruitment campaigns however, usually make use of several strategies.

## Using the media to your advantage

Your need to recruit staff may be driven by many factors:

● an expansion in demand for your goods or services

● an increased level of investment

● the introduction of new technology

● the re-location of your base

● the need to replace a long-serving member of staff who is about to retire.

These often make newsworthy stories for the local media. A simple

## Advertising Options

| | Word of Mouth | Display Cards | Jobcentre Ads | Freesheets | Newspapers Local | Newspapers Regional | Newspapers National | Magazines |
|---|---|---|---|---|---|---|---|---|
| Local Unskilled P/T | ✓ | ✓ | ✓ | ✓ | ✓ | | | |
| Local Unskilled F/T | ✓ | ✓ | ✓ | ✓ | ✓ | | | |
| General Skills P/T | ✓ | ✓ | ✓ | ✓ | ✓ | | | |
| General Skills F/T | ✓ | | ✓ | ✓ | ✓ | ✓ | | |
| Skilled Workers P/T | ✓ | | ✓ | ✓ | ✓ | ✓ | | |
| Skilled Workers F/T | ✓ | | ✓ | ✓ | ✓ | ✓ | ✓ | ✓ |
| Professional Staff P/T | ✓ | | | | | ✓ | ✓ | ✓ |
| Professional Staff F/T | ✓ | | | | | ✓ | ✓ | ✓ |

Fig.10. Appropriate advertising options for different types of staff.

press-release or a phone call to the newsdesk of your local paper, radio or TV station, can result in a story or report which puts your organisation in a good light and advertises your need for staff. It's a good means of advertising and it's free!

## ATTRACTING THE CANDIDATES

The purpose of an advertisement is to stimulate interest in the job you have to offer. So whatever strategy you choose remember to keep in mind the following rules:

- Keep your advertisement clear and simple.

- Use full words rather than abbreviations.

- Use the job description and the person specification to help you describe the job and the sort of person you are looking for.

- Say whether the job is full-time or part-time, shiftwork or regular hours, temporary or permanent.

- Tell readers how to obtain further details.

- Give an address, a telephone number and, if possible, the name of a contact person.

- Set a deadline for enquiries.

- Keep your options open. Preconceived notions about age, experience and gender could deter good candidates from applying.

### Remembering the readership

Your advertisement will be read by customers and clients alike. Try to ensure that it is compatible with the image your organisation is trying to project. If you are worried about security, or if you wish to remain anonymous you can arrange with magazines and newspapers to have a box number. Research however, suggests that the anonymous approach puts people off applying.

If your budget will allow more than just the minimum information in the advertisement, try to attract the more motivated candidates by emphasising aspects of the job which offer:

- interest
- prospects
- good earnings and/or security
- opportunities for personal involvement
- good working relationships
- opportunities for further training.

You wouldn't want to encourage applications from individuals who are attracted to the job because of anything other than a desire to work. So don't waste effort in describing:

- holidays
- opportunities for travel
- social facilities
- fringe benefits.

## HANDLING ENQUIRIES

A good advertising strategy will attract a great deal of interest. Unless your advertisement specifically tells readers to write for further details, or establishes times when they should telephone, you can expect the first enquiries within minutes of publication. You need to be prepared.

### Preparing an information pack

At this stage a significant number of enquiries will probably be unsuitable and may not develop into serious applications, so try to avoid wasting time and talking directly to callers. Far better to have an **information pack** ready by the telephone to send out to enquirers. If possible delegate this job to a receptionist or clerk. The pack could contain:

- a brief description of your organisation
- a job description
- an application form
- a 'receipt of application acknowledgement card' to be completed by the candidate
- a standard letter thanking the enquirer for his interest and setting a deadline for returning the completed application form.

Peace and quiet are essential when it comes to sifting through all the applications so, if possible, choose a Friday as your closing date. This enables you to take all the information away for the weekend. It also means that any applications delayed in the post, or sent too late, should be on your desk by Monday morning.

## PROCESSING APPLICATIONS

Forms sent out only a few days ago could be completed and on their way back to you by return of post, so you need to establish a system for processing and storing the incoming paperwork. Don't waste time worrying about the quality or quantity of applicants just yet. You've decided upon a closing date so, for the moment at least, concentrate on ensuring that the material is processed effectively and stored securely. In that way the recruitment process will not distract you from your main task of keeping the organisation working efficiently despite your staffing problems.

### Ensuring confidentiality

Bear in mind also that applicants put their trust in you to handle information with sensitivity and confidentiality. Many would not want their present employers to know of their interest in this job. Your staff and colleagues however, will be naturally curious to know who is applying, So, out of respect for your applicants, restrict access to information and keep details of applicants confidential. After the deadline you can share information with those staff and colleagues who need to know who has applied. Restricting access to applications also minimises the chances of losing part or all of an applicant's paperwork.

### Setting up simple procedures

Processing applications is really a matter of good, basic office practice. Get ahead of the game by:

- making sure that there is space available in a secure filing cabinet

- clearly marking a file with the job title and deadline on it

- having a checklist stapled inside the front cover (see Figure 11) listing the name of each candidate and the date you receive his application.

### Recording the progress of each application

Think also about the various stages in the recruitment process and make up another checklist (see Figure 12) which can be stapled to each applicant's information as it arrives. A simple 'tick box' system allows you

| JOB VACANCY | | |
|---|---|---|

| Name of Candidate | | Application Received |
|---|---|---|
| | | |
| | | |
| | | |
| | | |
| | | |
| | | |
| | | |
| | | |
| | | |
| | | |
| | | |
| | | |
| | | |
| | | |
| | | |
| | | |
| | | |
| | | |
| | | |
| | | |
| | | |
| | | |
| | | |
| | | |
| | | |
| | | |
| | | |
| | | |
| | | |
| | | |
| | | |
| | | |
| | | |
| | | |
| | | |
| | | |
| | | |
| | | |
| | | |

Fig. 11. A checklist for recording candidates' names
and date of receipt of application.

| JOB VACANCY |
| --- |

Name of Candidate _____

Application Received _____ / _____ / _____

Acknowledgement Sent _____ / _____ / _____

References Requested _____ / _____ / _____

References Received (1) _____ / _____ / _____

(2) _____ / _____ / _____


Shortlisted ☐ Yes ☐ No

Invited to Interview _____ / _____ / _____

Accepted Invitation ☐ Yes ☐ No

Offered Job ☐ Yes ☐ No

Regret Letter Sent _____ / _____ / _____

Contract Issued _____ / _____ / _____

Contract Returned _____ / _____ / _____

Start Date _____ / _____ / _____

Fig. 12. Checklist for recording the recruitment process
for individual candidates.

to record your dealings with each applicant and keep a track of the state of play. A well thought out checklist can record a candidate's involvement in the entire recruitment process. It can record:

- the date an application was received
- any acknowledgements sent
- if references have been taken up
- if references have been received
- if the candidate has been shortlisted
- if any standard 'sorry' letters have been sent
- if the candidate has been invited to attend interview
- if the candidate has been offered the job
- if he has accepted the offer
- if a contract has been issued
- if a contract has been signed and returned.

### Acknowledging applications

Selecting staff is a logical and sequential process. It begins by ensuring that every candidate's application is acknowledged. The receipt of application acknowledgement card (see Figure 13) which you sent out to applicants for them to complete, can now be returned to them in a plain envelope. Applicants should get a good impression of your organisation even if you don't intend to employ them.

---

For acknowledgement, please complete below and write your name and address overleaf

                        CI Systems Ltd

                                        42–44 the Broadway
                                        Earl Shilton
                                        Nottingham
                                        SW7 4KY


Application for the post of ...................................................................

Dear Applicant,

I acknowledge receipt of your application for the above post. It will be considered shortly.

                        Yours faithfully,

                                        B. Johnson,

                                        Managing Director.

---

Fig. 13. Receipt of application acknowledgement card.

## IDENTIFYING THE EVIDENCE

It isn't unusual for an organisation to receive 60 or 70 applications for a job. Some will be unsuitable but others will appear to have some or all of the skills and qualities you require. Some candidates will have sent you exactly what you asked for. Others will have added impressive looking CVs, photographs, and testimonials from previous employers. Understandably, there is always a temptation to look more favourably on the glossy, carefully prepared applications at the expense of the more subdued documents. Somehow though, you need to get an objective initial view of the apparent strengths and weaknesses of each candidate. Underneath the gloss, or between the lines, there must be **evidence of suitability** to support your further interest in an applicant.

It is a sad fact of life that the *best person* for a job is not always successful in his job applications. Companies tend to recruit the *best candidate*, the person who impresses them most. They assume that the best person and the best candidate are one and the same – they are not. Jobhunting is a skill which can be learned like any other. Many people can write glowing letters of application and produce polished, professional looking CVs. They can also shine at interview, but their skills at applying for and securing jobs may far outweigh their ability to actually *do* the job.

### Establishing a scoresheet for candidates

With such a lot of information to digest it is almost guaranteed that by the time you have read the tenth application, you won't remember anything about the first one. So, spend some time beforehand, revisiting the job description and person specification. From those two documents it should be quite easy to set up a simple score sheet so that you can record the apparent strengths and weaknesses of each candidate.

## SCORING AND CHECKING

Figure 14 is a job description for an Office Manager in a medium-sized transport company. Figure 15 is a simple scoresheet which was used to identify candidates who, on paper at least, appeared to have the necessary attributes to meet the requirements of the job. It is based on the topics used to construct the person specification described in Figure 7 in Chapter 2.

As each application was read, the manager looked for evidence of:

# Carter Transport Ltd

## Job Description

**Job Title:**    Office Manager

**Reports To:**    Managing Director

1. **Purpose of the Job**

   To manage the office, and the administrative functions of the company, including secretarial and domestic services, to ensure an efficient service to managers, clients and members of the public.

2. **Principal Accountabilities**

   (a) Manage a team of clerical, secretarial, and administrative staff responsible for word processing, filing, ordering and despatching, vehicle scheduling, invoicing, handling mail, switchboard and reception.

   (b) Ensure an efficient and effective transport booking service for current customers and members of the general public.

   (c) Produce weekly transport schedules and monthly statistical information for senior management.

   (d) Maintain an appropriate level of company insurance and administer claims for vehicle damage, contents and personal accident.

   (e) Establish systems for the purchasing of all office material, identifying and negotiating with local suppliers to ensure value for money.

   (f) Supervise cleaning staff to ensure the maintenance of standards in the administrative and public areas.

   (g) Any other administrative or managerial duties appropriate to the skills and experience of the job holder which may be identified by the managing director.

3. **Knowledge and Experience Required**

   Substantial administrative experience, and a proven track record in the management of staff are essential requirements for this post.

   Excellent computer and word processing skills are also essential, together with a broad knowledge of filing systems, telephone switchboards, fax machines and other office equipment.

   The successful candidate should have the ability to communicate effectively at all levels.

   A level of education equivalent to NVQ level 4 in business administration is required. Education to a similar level in other related subjects however, will also be acceptable.

   Experience of training administrative staff is desirable and, as this post is considered to be an excellent position for career development within the company, the motivation to work towards a further management qualification would be an advantage.

Fig. 14. A job description for an office manager in a transport company.

**Carter Transport Ltd**
**Candidate Scoresheet**

| Score | Candidate 1 | | | Candidate 2 | | | Candidate 3 | | |
|---|---|---|---|---|---|---|---|---|---|
| | 1 | 2 | 3 | 1 | 2 | 3 | 1 | 2 | 3 |
| Qualifications, knowledge | | | | | | | | | |
| Specific skills | | | | | | | | | |
| Relevant experience | | | | | | | | | |
| Personal attributes | | | | | | | | | |
| Physical attributes | | | | | | | | | |
| Added value | | | | | | | | | |

| Score | Candidate 4 | | | Candidate 5 | | | Candidate 6 | | |
|---|---|---|---|---|---|---|---|---|---|
| | 1 | 2 | 3 | 1 | 2 | 3 | 1 | 2 | 3 |
| Qualifications, knowledge | | | | | | | | | |
| Specific skills | | | | | | | | | |
| Relevant experience | | | | | | | | | |
| Personal attributes | | | | | | | | | |
| Physical attributes | | | | | | | | | |
| Added value | | | | | | | | | |

| Score | Candidate 7 | | | Candidate 8 | | | Candidate 9 | | |
|---|---|---|---|---|---|---|---|---|---|
| | 1 | 2 | 3 | 1 | 2 | 3 | 1 | 2 | 3 |
| Qualifications, knowledge | | | | | | | | | |
| Specific skills | | | | | | | | | |
| Relevant experience | | | | | | | | | |
| Personal attributes | | | | | | | | | |
| Physical attributes | | | | | | | | | |
| Added value | | | | | | | | | |

Fig. 15. A scoresheet for identifying candidates who meet the job description specifications.

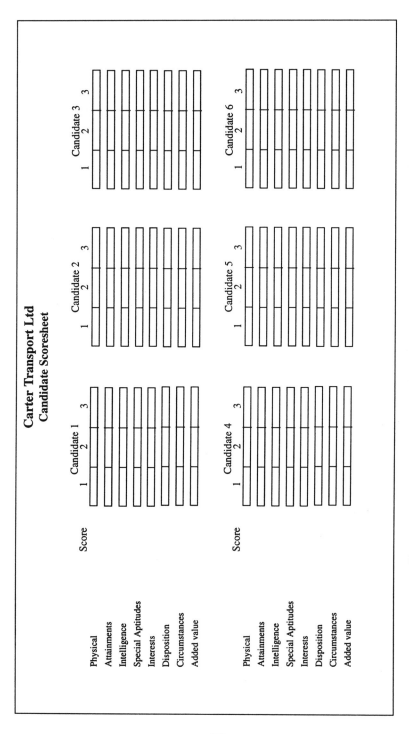

Fig. 16. Candidate scoresheet based on the seven-point plan person specification.

- qualifications
- specific skills
- relevant experience
- personal attributes
- physical attributes.

A tick in **column 1** against 'qualifications' indicated that the candidate did not appear to have achieved the general level of education which was required. In the case of the office manager post, the company had decided that five A–C grades at GCSE or equivalent, including English and maths, were the baseline essential qualifications. A tick in **column 2** indicated that the candidate had achieved the required standard, while a tick in **column 3** showed that the candidate had achieved more than the baseline requirement.

Similarly, a tick in **column 1** against 'relevant experience' indicated that there was no evidence that the candidate could use the full range of office equipment described in the 'knowledge and experience' section of the job description. A tick in **column 3** suggested that the candidate probably had more than the baseline requirement of skill in this area.

### Drawing conclusions

At the end of the scoring exercise, any candidate who scored **1** in any of the four categories was rejected. Clearly they didn't have the full range of qualifications, skills and experience required to do the job.

Ten candidates were found to have scored **2** or above against the four requirements and, of those, the five with the most scores in **column 3** were put on the shortlist.

Figure 16 is a similar scoresheet based on the person specification constructed from the seven-point plan described in Chapter 2.

- Physical attributes
- Attainments
- Intelligence
- Special aptitudes
- Interests
- Disposition
- Circumstances.

## RECOGNISING ADDED VALUE

Look again at both scoresheets. Each has a category marked **added**

**value.** It is there for you to record any special skills which a candidate may be offering over and above those which you have identified as being important for the fulfilment of the job. For example:

● One candidate may be able to speak French. This may not be an essential skill for the fulfilment of the job today, but if your plans to expand into Europe come to anything, a French-speaking member of staff may be just what you need.

● Another candidate may have previous experience in book-keeping. You aren't looking to recruit a book-keeper, but when your existing member of staff retires in two years, this may just give you the degree of flexibility needed to restructure the administration of your company.

● A third candidate may have had previous experience in a company well known for its ability to meet seemingly impossible deadlines. This may be an aspect of your activities which you would like to improve. It's not in the job description but, by importing someone with the right attitude and know-how, it might just be enough to raise awareness and start making steps in that direction.

Recognising the added value that a candidate could bring to your company, is not in itself a reason for offering that person a job. Primarily your choice of candidate should be driven by his ability to fulfil the requirements of the job, and his potential to contribute to the development of your organisation in the future. Often though, as in the case above, you will find that several applicants appear able to meet all your basic requirements. At that stage, you can start to shop around and consider what's in the added value column.

## SHORTLISTING

An exercise like the one described above should allow you to sort applications into three distinct groups:

● those who are clearly unsuitable
● those whose suitability is unclear, possibly requiring further investigation
● those who should definitely be placed on the shortlist.

In effect you should be able to reduce that pile of 60 or 70 applications to a long shortlist of six or seven (ten at most) candidates who appear to have all or most of the skills and qualities you're looking for.

One or two will be strong in all areas, others may be less strong in certain aspects but they may have been included because of the added value they could bring to your company.

## Sorting out the remaining applicants
The remainder will fit into two categories.

- Those who are clearly not suitable to your needs. You can send these people an immediate, short but sympathetic letter of regret. Something along the lines of the example in Figure 17 should do.

- Borderline applicants who probably need further consideration. The degree of ruthlessness with which you treat these will depend upon the strength and number of candidates you have already decided should be interviewed. With five or six strong candidates, you needn't spend too much time on the 'maybes'. On the other hand, with only one or two strong candidates, it would be sensible to look again at the 'maybes' to see if there is anything you may have overlooked.

*Double checking*
If you alone are responsible for the shortlisting, it may be worthwhile asking a colleague to carry out the same scoring and checking exercise to discover whether he supports your opinions.

## GETTING EVIDENCE FROM ELSEWHERE

With strong interest in six or seven candidates it is time to begin collecting evidence from elsewhere. Some evidence may already have been sent to you.

## Considering testimonials
Some candidates include **testimonials** from previous employers within their initial application. Testimonials are easily obtained and they always describe the subject in a positive light. They aren't worth much and they shouldn't be considered as valid evidence. Few employers are going to give a person a critical testimonial and, even if they did, only an idiot would include such criticism in an application for a job.

**Smallworld Removals**
**15–17 Grange Road**
**South Woodford**
**Northumberland**
**NE7 2TW**

**Tel: 01976 94437**

13/3/9X

Dear Mr Blake

Thank you for applying for a post as a driver for this company.

We have had a good response to our advertisment and, as there are a number of applicants who more closely match our requirements, we do not propose to include your name on the shortlist for the post.

We thank you for your interest however, and wish you every success in your search for a new position.

Yours sincerely

James Johnson
**Fleet Manager**

Fig. 17. Letter of regret to an unsuccessful applicant.

## Understanding records of achievement

Young candidates, just out of school or college, may send their **record of achievement** as evidence of their hard work and integrity. Like testimonials they are essentially in the control of the candidate, and therefore it's difficult to treat the information they contain as objective. Well kept, carefully collated records of achievement can be a pleasure to read. The information they contain, however, is determined not by the school or college, but by the young people themselves who are free to include or exclude anything they want. Like testimonials therefore, it would be difficult to imagine how such documents could contain anything but positive statements. Records of achievement are useful however, if you decide to interview young candidates. Young people straight out of school or college have little previous experience of work or life to draw upon and therefore they can be difficult to engage in conversation. At interview, the record of achievement can be an icebreaker; a useful focus for initial discussion.

## Taking up references

References are documents concerning a candidate's suitability for the post you advertise. They are written to you in confidence. Their contents should never be disclosed to a candidate either by you or by their author. Anything resembling a reference but which a candidate sends to you is, in fact, a testimonial and it deserves little credence.

Most employers ask applicants to supply the names and addresses of at least two people who could act as referees on their behalf. Ideally, one of the two referees should be able to comment on a candidate's work record, while the other should be able to supply more general information about the candidate's character. While, on the face of it, it would seem perfectly reasonable to expect that one referee should be the applicant's present employer, many applicants have legitimate reasons for asking you not to contact that person until much later in the process.

Despite the above, references remain somewhat controversial. They are considered to be useful sources of information because:

- they are confidential

- they are written by people who know the candidate well

- they can paint a broader picture of the candidate

- they can support or deny statements made by the candidate in his application.

## Carter Transport Ltd
### Reference Questionnaire

Name: _____

Position Applied for: _____

Main Duties and Responsibilities: _____

_____

Please give me your assessment of this person's ability to successfully undertake the above job by completing the questionnaire below.

Currently, what is your assessment of the candidate's:

|  | Very Good | Good | Fair | Poor |
|---|---|---|---|---|
| Quality of work | | | | |
| Quantity of work | | | | |
| Application to the job | | | | |
| Relations with others | | | | |
| Management skills | | | | |
| Attendance/Punctuality | | | | |
| Health Record | | | | |
| People Skills | | | | |
| Teamwork | | | | |
| Work without Supervision | | | | |

Would you re-employ?     Yes/No

Name: _____Position: _____

Signature: _____Date: _____

Fig. 18. An example of a reference questionnaire.

74

On the other hand, critics argue that:

● References may not be as confidential as they appear. Undoubtedly, some referees show them to candidates before they are sent.

● As with testimonials, the applicant chooses his referees. It is unlikely he would suggest anyone who would have negative statements to make.

● The writer has to trust the reader to keep his confidence. Many referees prefer to omit information rather than make negative statements. In effect therefore, references are easy to misinterpret.

● There are dishonest employers who will produce excellent references for poor members of staff whom they would like to lose.

● By the same token, employers may be less enthusiastic in describing the skills and qualities of staff whom they wish to keep.

Despite their limitations, you should always take up references on anyone you are considering interviewing. The evidence may be dubious, but it is *evidence* all the same.

### Strengthening the value of references
References are strongest when they address a candidate's ability to carry out a specific job. In order to avoid pointless platitudes such as: 'I'm sure John Smith will be a credit to any organisation lucky enough to recruit him', make a point of sending referees a copy of the job description and asking them to comment on John Smith's ability to carry out the duties described.

### Using questionnaires
Some of the drawbacks mentioned above can be overcome by sending **questionnaires** for referees to complete. By asking specific questions, employers are able to ensure that referees address issues and make definite statements. Many employers feel that the quality of information obtained from a questionnaire is greatly superior to that of a general reference. An example of a reference questionnaire is given in Figure 18.

## MAKING THE FINAL SHORTLIST

How much time do you have? Classic textbooks will tell you to look at the references before determining the final shortlist. Referees however, need time to respond to your enquiries, and therefore, waiting for their response before calling candidates to interview can be a lengthy process. There are three options available to you.

1.   You could take a decision now and invite all your current shortlisted candidates to participate in the next phase of the recruitment process, but you run the risk of inviting someone to interview who will obtain poor references and waste some of your time.

2.   You could wait until you have received all responses before producing your final shortlist one or two weeks from now.

3.   You could speed up the process by telephoning referees and sending questionnaires by fax.

## Choosing your options

Only you can decide how best to proceed at this stage. If you choose the third option however, bear in mind that you may need to give referees some thinking time. Telephone them, let them know that you are seeking information about an applicant for a job and then arrange to telephone again later, by which time they will be better prepared to answer your questions.

## SUMMARY

● Most companies have to advertise to attract the right candidates. There are several options available. For the best chance of success, don't put all your eggs in one basket, use a range of appropriate advertising strategies.

● Keep your advertisement clear and simple. Use full words, state the nature of the employment, and tell readers how to obtain further details. Set a deadline for enquiries. Attract the more motivated candidates by emphasising positive aspects of the job, rather than the fringe benefits.

● Prepare for enquiries by having a package of information ready to send out.

● Processing applications is a matter of good, basic office practice. Be prepared to receive, store, and respond to applications. Ensure confidentiality by restricting access to information.

- Some candidates will be highly skilled job-hunters. Their applications will be impressive. Make sure your shortlisting process is based on *evidence* rather than neatness and *gloss*. The *best candidate* is not always the *best person* for a job.

- When shortlisting, sort candidates into three distinct groups: (1) those who are clearly unsuitable (2) those whose suitability is unclear (3) those who should definitely be placed on the shortlist.

- Always take up references on candidates who you feel may be suitable for interview. If you doubt the accuracy of references try using a questionnaire instead.

- Time is always an important factor in recruitment. You can speed up the process by using the telephone and fax to obtain references.

## CASE STUDIES

### John's great plans fall apart

Having stressed the need to trawl far and wide for the best staff he could find, John is initially pleased to be given a generous advertising budget for his replacement staff. He advertises widely and is pleased with the level of response.

He keeps most of the completed application forms in his pending tray on top of his desk, except for those who, at first glance, seem to be particularly promising. These, he takes home to read each evening as they arrive.

A week after the closing date however, he is very embarrassed to receive a call from an irate candidate who wants to know how his present employer has discovered that he had applied for the job. John can only surmise that someone has glanced into his pending tray and has mentioned what he saw to a friend. It's a small world!

The following week, at a shortlisting meeting, he discovers that he has lost an application from a particularly strong candidate. He took it home two weeks ago. It might still be there; or in his car, or . . .

### Trish orders her priorities

Running the department is hard enough when you are understaffed. Trish doesn't want to spend time worrying about the exact wording of an advertisement so she asks her secretary to prepare a suitable advertisement, place it in the local newspaper, and be ready to deal with the enquiries that follow.

Diana, Trish's secretary has a flair for organisation and so she is well prepared for enquiries. Unfortunately, they are few and largely inappropriate. The advertisement is far too small and badly located within the newspaper. Trish needs applicants who are qualified and experienced and the advertisement fails to mention this. As a result, many of the enquirers are college-leavers seeking to gain initial experience, or people looking to change their career direction.

## Mark makes a long-term investment

As far as Mark is concerned, every appointment is a long-term investment in the company, and bringing the 'right' person into the team is a matter of personal pride. With a key player missing, life isn't easy but there can be no guarantee that things will improve unless he can attract the right person for that job. He spends a couple of evenings writing the advertisement, deciding where it should be placed, and establishing the system for processing applications. Then he returns to the task of keeping the business running and covering the gap in his organisation. On the closing date, he is pleasantly surprised at the strength and quality of applications he has received.

## DISCUSSION POINTS

1. Should the person who wrote the job description and person specification also write the advertisement for the job?

2. What information do you need in order to establish the best advertising strategy?

3. Which aspects of the recruitment process can you delegate to others and which should you take care of yourself?

4. How can you ensure confidentiality?

5. What evidence will you be looking for when it comes to shortlisting your candidates?

6. Will you rely upon your own opinion or should you seek the views of a trusted colleague?

7. Will you ask for general references or send out questionnaires?

# 4
# Making the Final Selection

## CREATING AN EVENT

Having chosen your shortlist and determined how you are going to take up references, it's time to set about creating a **final selection event**. This usually involves inviting your shortlisted applicants to attend an interview. In the past, this single, formal discussion between employer and candidate, would have been regarded as the most important component of the whole recruitment and selection process. Frequently, following a brief telephone call, it was the only component in the process. Today, although it remains important, it is more usual to regard the job interview as part of a much wider process of gathering evidence of suitability for a job. So far you may have gathered evidence from:

- completed application forms
- letters of application
- CVs.

Some of the claims made by candidates will have been supported by referees but at this stage, although there may be a clear front-runner, it is unlikely that you will have all the information you need to make your final selection. At this stage also, it frequently becomes clear that a simple interview will not provide you with all the evidence you need to feel confident in making your decision. Candidates for a secretarial post for example, may be able to offer typing and word processing qualifications as evidence of skill. But what of their ability to prepare routine letters on behalf of the employer? An interview is not the best way to discover their skills in this area. It is far better to establish a simple test to be done before the formal interview takes place. For this reason, the final selection process may have several components and that is why it is best described as an **event**.

### Writing regret letters
First of all however, it is time to write to any other applicants who have

**All Occasions Catering**
**Unit 17**
**Fenland Industrial Estate**
**Boston-on-Wold**
**Lincolnshire**
**LN5 9TS**

**Tel: 01987 342765**

16/7/9X

Dear Mr Johnson

Thank you for applying for the post of confectionery assistant within our company.

We have had a good response to our advertisement and, as there are a number of applicants who appear to more closely match our requirements, we have decided not to invite you for interview on this occasion.

I should like to thank you for your interest in working at AOC however, and I wish you every success in your search for a new position.


Yours sincerely


Mrs S White
**Personnel and Administration Manager**

Fig. 19. An example of a letter to an applicant who has not been shortlisted for interview.

not now been included on the shortlist. A simple letter along the lines of the one in Figure 19 is all that is required. Simply thank applicants for their interest in the post and let them know that, on this occasion, their application was not successful. It is rarely useful to enter into deeper correspondence about why you chose not to select a certain candidate.

Shortly it will be necessary to invite your shortlisted candidates to the selection event but before you do, spend a little time thinking about selection tests and other devices you can use to improve the quality of the evidence you can collect. How you structure the event will determine what you say to candidates in your invitation to them.

## USING SELECTION TESTS

There are a variety of tests used to identify differences between people and their suitability for different types of job. Some tests are highly sophisticated while others can be set up easily by any employer. The more sophisticated tests, sometimes referred to as **psychometric tests**, are usually prepared by specialists for particular purposes and cannot easily be adapted to different situations. These tests can also be expensive to develop and use.

### Using personality tests
Personality tests are not really *tests* at all. In truth they should be referred to as *personality questionnaires*. Their purpose is to identify polarities of personality. They'll indicate, for example, whether a candidate is an introvert or an extrovert, independent or dependent, tough minded or tender minded, and whether the candidate has a high or low degree of self confidence.

### Using interest tests
Like personality tests, **interest tests** are not *tests* at all. They indicate *interests*. There is no pass or fail mark. Their purpose is to assess whether a person has more interest in one particular area of work than another. Presumably, a person working within their area of interest will be more highly motivated than one who is in an area of work which holds little personal interest. Typically, these tests group candidates into those with specific or technical interests, those with concern for people, and those with an interest in arts and design, or data and systems.

In recruitment and selection, the use of interest tests is somewhat limited. Generally there is a feeling that they are easy to fake. An applicant for a job in the caring professions for example, will always try to respond to questions in such a way that his interest in people is highlighted.

## Using psychometric tests

It is beyond the scope of this book to go into detail about **psychometric tests**, except to highlight the fact that they are available should you require them. Such tests are useful in situations where you need to identify likely candidates for a fairly standard job from a large number of applicants. The armed forces, the police, the prison service and some types of apprenticeship schemes, all use such tests.

- They could be of use to you if you are looking to open a new branch of your activity in a totally new location, a new supermarket for example. In such cases they could be used as an initial screening process for identifying 50 local people to staff the new project.

- They could also be of use if your organisation is of a size where you regularly appoint people to standard posts. Local authorities, the health services and the civil service for example, have a constant need for people with general administrative skills to replace staff leaving through retirement, promotion, or ill health. The scale of recruitment activity is such that an investment in these tests could be justified.

## Using attainment tests

**Attainment tests** try to measure a candidate's ability by assessing their skill and knowledge. Applicants for clerical jobs, for example, may be given tests in simple arithmetic, spelling or grammar. Tests such as these are a more reliable indication of a candidate's ability to do the job than old, school examination results. From the candidate's point of view, although such tests may seem rather daunting, they offer the chance to demonstrate skill in a very practical way, especially if the candidate has no formal qualifications in this area. From your point of view it is much better to *test* for levels of skill than to *talk* about such skills at an interview.

## Designing work sample tests (simulations)

Sometimes referred to as 'performance tests', **work sample tests** are the easiest tests to develop and administer and you don't need to employ a team of psychologists or recruitment specialists in order to do so. Essentially the tests can be created by devising a simple practical

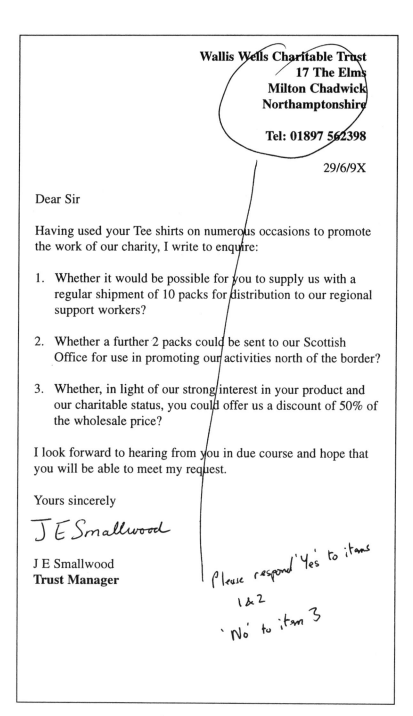

**Wallis Wells Charitable Trust**
**17 The Elms**
**Milton Chadwick**
**Northamptonshire**

**Tel: 01897 562398**

29/6/9X

Dear Sir

Having used your Tee shirts on numerous occasions to promote the work of our charity, I write to enquire:

1. Whether it would be possible for you to supply us with a regular shipment of 10 packs for distribution to our regional support workers?

2. Whether a further 2 packs could be sent to our Scottish Office for use in promoting our activities north of the border?

3. Whether, in light of our strong interest in your product and our charitable status, you could offer us a discount of 50% of the wholesale price?

I look forward to hearing from you in due course and hope that you will be able to meet my request.

Yours sincerely

*J E Smallwood*

J E Smallwood
**Trust Manager**

*Please respond 'Yes' to items 1 & 2 'No' to item 3*

Fig. 20. Example of a performance test for the post of secretary.

Book-keeping exercise: Please complete this bank reconciliation sheet to reflect the bank statement and accounts sheet following

## Smiths Fresh Foods No 4 Account

Account No.

### Bank Reconciliation Form

| | £ | P |
|---|---|---|
| Balance as per bank statement | | |
| *31/3   *30/6   *30/9   *31/12 | | |

* delete where necessary

Less: Cheques not yet presented

| Date Drawn | Cheque No | Payee | £ | P |
|---|---|---|---|---|
| | | | | |
| | | | | |
| | | | | |
| | | | | |
| | | | | |
| | | | | |
| | | | | |
| | | | | |

Balance per book *31/3   *30/6   *30/9   *31/12
* delete where necessary

Certified Correct   Signature......................................

Position Held ..............................

date ...............................................

NOTES: 1. The above form should be completed at the end of March, June, September and December.
2. Any discrepancy should be notified to accounts within one month of the date shown in Note 1.

Fig. 21. Example of a bank reconciliation problem for the post of book-keeper.

**Midway Bank plc**
Town Branch, Library Place
Cambridge
Smiths Fresh Foods No 4 Account

| 1996 | Sheet 67 | Account No 71036549 | | | | |
|---|---|---|---|---|---|---|
| | | | Debit | Credit | Balance | |
| | | | | | Credit C | Debit D |
| Dec-31 | Balance Brought Forward | | | | 12.94 | C |
| 1995 | | | | | | |
| Jan-16 | Sundries | | | 300.65 | 313.59 | C |
| Jan-17 | 100365 | | 50.00 | | 263.59 | C |
| Jan-18 | 100369 | | 37.78 | | 225.81 | C |
| Jan-22 | 100366 | | 8.57 | | | |
| Jan-22 | 100367 | | 20.54 | | | |
| Jan-22 | 100368 | | 12.50 | | 184.20 | C |
| Jan-23 | 100371 | | 24.79 | | 159.41 | C |
| Jan-28 | 100370 | | 9.40 | | 150.01 | C |
| Jan-30 | 100373 | | 46.00 | | 104.01 | C |
| Feb-01 | 100375 | | 50.00 | | | |
| Feb-01 | Sundries | | | 292.4 | 346.41 | C |
| Feb-05 | 100374 | | 30.00 | | 316.41 | C |
| Feb-12 | 100376 | | 14.98 | | 301.43 | C |
| Feb-15 | 100378 | | 6.25 | | | |
| Feb-15 | 100379 | | 16.11 | | 279.07 | C |
| Feb-19 | 100372 | | 46.03 | | | |
| Feb-19 | 100380 | | 4.50 | | 228.54 | C |
| Feb 21 | 100382 | | 5.00 | | 223.54 | C |
| Mar-5 | 100385 | | 50.00 | | 173.54 | C |
| Mar-8 | 100381 | | 35.00 | | 138.54 | C |
| Mar-15 | 100383 | | 34.60 | | 103.94 | C |
| Mar-22 | Sundries | | | 251.86 | 355.80 | C |
| Mar-26 | 000003 | | 25.17 | | 330.63 | C |
| Mar-28 | Balance Carried Forward | | | | 330.63 | C |

Please refer to Customer Information printed overleaf, and then file away safely.

| Smiths Fresh Foods No 4 Account | | | | | | |
|---|---|---|---|---|---|---|
| Date | Cheque No | Details | Amount | Paid in | Balance | |
| | | Balance brought forward | | | 12.94 | |
| 1996 | | | | | | |
| 16-Jan | | Cheque paid into bank | | 300.65 | 313.59 | |
| 16-Jan | 100365 | Walkers Ltd | 50.00 | | 263.59 | |
| 16-Jan | 100366 | Besco | 8.57 | | 255.02 | |
| 18-Jan | 100367 | Collins Ltd | 20.54 | | 234.48 | |
| 18-Jan | 100368 | Carters | 12.50 | | 221.98 | |
| 18-Jan | 100369 | Northern Buses | 37.78 | | 184.20 | |
| 20-Jan | 100370 | Boom Bros | 9.40 | | 174.80 | |
| 20-Jan | 100371 | Smart Tec | 24.79 | | 150.01 | |
| 25-Jan | 100372 | Alpine systems | 46.03 | | 103.98 | |
| 25-Jan | 100373 | B &G discs | 46.00 | | 57.98 | |
| 01-Feb | | Cheque paid into bank | | 292.40 | 350.38 | |
| 01-Feb | 100374 | Normans | 30.00 | | 320.38 | |
| 01-Feb | 100375 | Water Co | 50.00 | | 270.38 | |
| 05-Feb | 100376 | Besco | 14.98 | | 255.40 | |
| 05-Feb | 100377 | Electricity | 20.00 | | 235.40 | |
| 08-Feb | 100378 | Carteres | 6.25 | | 229.15 | |
| 08-Feb | 100379 | Collins | 16.11 | | 213.04 | |
| 08-Feb | 100380 | Shell | 4.50 | | 208.54 | |
| 10-Feb | 100381 | Smiths Systems | 35.00 | | 173.54 | |
| 15-Feb | 100382 | Carter Woodworking International | 5.00 | | 168.54 | |
| 01-Mar | 100383 | Fortuna | 34.60 | | 133.94 | |
| 01-Mar | 100384 | Lune Bleu transportation | 40.00 | | 93.94 | |
| 02-Mar | 100385 | Excel Microshares | 50.00 | | 43.94 | |
| 07-Mar | 000001 | Florence Co Ltd | 10.00 | | 33.94 | |
| 10-Mar | 000002 | Breem Bros | 30.00 | | 3.94 | |
| 22-Mar | | Cheque paid into bank | | 251.86 | 255.80 | |
| 23-Mar | 000003 | Carter International Woodworking | 25.17 | | 230.63 | |

Fig. 21. Continued.

85

exercise based upon the realities of the job. You can take examples from actual events, or you can set up realistic situations which simulate the types of problems and situations likely to be encountered in the job.

## Examples

*Designing tests in manual jobs*
Often it is possible to break a job down to one or two skills which provide the key to success. A waiter or waitress in a restaurant, for example, should be able to carry a certain number of plates and move among the tables with confidence. Applicants for machinist jobs in a clothing factory may be unfamiliar with the workings of your particular make of machine, but they should be able to thread a needle and produce a variety of neat hand stitches on a sample of material. An applicant for a warehouse job should be able to stack a pallet in such a way that items are securely interlocked. Perhaps they should also be able to check for damage, and repackage items if required. Maybe it would also be worthwhile asking candidates to drive a forklift truck along a set course.

*Testing secretarial skills*
Figure 20 is a simple performance test for a post of secretary to the managing director of a medium-sized manufacturing company in the Midlands. The job description required the post-holder to be able to respond to routine enquiries. In this case, the test required candidates to respond to a query from a charitable trust politely but negatively.

Candidates were offered a choice of personal computer or a typewriter in order to make their response. The resulting letter was checked by the interviewing panel for the appropriateness of the response, layout and accuracy of English. A careful note was taken of the time each candidate spent in producing the letter and their preferences for using the PC or typewriter was recorded. The ease with which they undertook the task and their response to the request to take the test was noted.

*Book-keeping*
Figure 21 is a simple book-keeping reconciliation problem. Once again, a great deal can be learned about a person's suitability for a particular post by asking them to undertake a sample of the duties which would be required of them.

*Using an in-tray exercise*
In-tray exercises are useful in the selection of candidates for middle and

senior management posts. Having explained the duties and responsibilities of the post, and given candidates a briefing on the present problems and priorities within your organisation, it is a fairly easy task to fill an in-tray with a range of letters, reports, and memos.

Some of the items will require urgent attention, while others can be left for weekend reading. Some issues arising from the in-tray can be delegated to junior staff, while others need to be brought to the urgent attention of senior managers. One or two items should require immediate written responses from candidates.

Candidates can be marked according to their level of clear thinking and the way they prioritise their work, delegate responsibility, handle urgent items of business, operate under stress, and respond in writing to specific questions.

*Requesting reports*
Does the job you wish to fill require the job-holder to write reports? If so, why not consider asking each shortlisted candidate to write a report and bring it along to the interview, or send it to you along with their acceptance to attend? Use a real situation to give candidates the background material and ask them to report on how they would solve the particular problem. At worst you'll gain the benefit of some creative solutions and at best you may find that the person with the best answer also turns out to be the best candidate at interview – in which case, your problems are solved. You may find that you have killed several birds with one stone.

*Asking candidates to make presentations*
Does the job require presentation skills? If so, you could build a presentation into the interview session. Ask candidates to prepare a 15 minute presentation on an issue of particular importance to the job. How would they reorganise the transport fleet? How could they establish a staff training plan and policy? How would they establish a sales development strategy?

What if the successful candidate needs to display skills in both report writing and presentation? Then, it is quite reasonable to ask shortlisted applicants to write a report and prepare a presentation. Some candidates may withdraw their application when faced with such a challenge, but that is not such a bad thing. Presumably, their withdrawal would be because they found the task too daunting, or because they couldn't be bothered to make the effort. In either case, you wouldn't have wanted to appoint them, so interviewing them would have wasted your time.

## THINKING ABOUT INTERVIEWS

**Interviews** are just about the final stage in the process of gathering and testing evidence about a candidate's suitability for a job. They give you the chance to get to know the person behind the application form and see how his approach will fit in with that of your organisation. No two interviews are the same, different organisations have different methods and procedures. Some have no methods at all!

### Holding preliminary interviews

Sometimes, if for example, you still have a longer shortlist than you would prefer at this stage, you could hold **preliminary interviews** to 'screen out' unlikely candidates and achieve a more manageable shortlist. You can do this yourself, or if your organisation has personnel staff, you can ask them to screen candidates for you. Be careful though to brief them well.

### Interviewing by telephone

Sometimes, the screening out interview can be done by telephone. From your point of view, it saves time and is considerably cheaper than a face-to-face meeting. Telephone interviews are not easy however, and they don't give you a great deal of evidence on which to base your judgement of a person. You cannot see the candidate and so you have to rely on your interpretation of the sound of his voice, his tone, intonation, and use of language. It demands skill to carry out a telephone interview so it isn't a method to be considered unless you are confident in your ability.

## CHOOSING YOUR INTERVIEW OPTIONS

With your final shortlist, you have three broad interview options open to you:

● one-to-one
● panel interviews
● sequential interviews.

### One-to-one

The simplest selection interview, often favoured by small companies, is the **one-to-one** meeting between you and the candidate. When they work out well these interviews are the closest thing to a natural conversation. They can be pleasant relaxed affairs *but* they can go badly wrong.

Some interviewers, for example, have trouble seeing beyond their first impressions of a person, and so their decisions can easily be biased in favour of a particular type of person. In a one-to-one interview the best candidate for a job may be overlooked in favour of one who more closely mirrors the interviewer's bias.

## Panel interviews

**Panel interviews** in which candidates face a group of interviewers are popular because they reduce the possibility of personal idiosyncrasies clouding the decision. Supporters of panel interviews argue that they enable an organisation to gain a broader insight into a candidate and take a more comprehensive view of his suitability for the post.

Arranging a panel interview involves the coordination of busy diaries, so it is customary for interview panels to see shortlisted candidates in one session, making the decision about who will be offered the job when the last candidate has been seen. To work well however, members of interviewing panels need to meet well before the event in order to agree each panel member's particular area of interest and to agree the sequence of questioning and the way the interview will be managed. Generally speaking, panel interviews need to have a recognised chairman who will direct the event.

## Sequential interviews

Many organisations use a **sequence** of separate interviews to arrive at their final choice of candidate. Sequential interviewing enables you to expose candidates to a wide range of interviewers who may use each interview to concentrate upon particular aspects of the job or particular qualities which will be required of the successful candidate. This method enables you to gain a great deal of knowledge about candidates, ensuring that the final decision is made in the light of a wide range of opinion.

## STRUCTURING THE EVENT

From the above, it should be clear that the final stage of selecting a candidate is not simply a matter of casually calling shortlisted candidates together for an interview. First of all you must structure the event by deciding which tests, if any, you are going to apply to candidates, and what form of interview you feel would be most appropriate in this instance.

## Using sophisticated systems

Generally speaking, the more senior posts in an organisation will require a higher level of management skill and a broader base of knowledge and experience. When recruiting to such posts, sequential interviews can be used alongside selection tests to create a highly sophisticated recruitment process known as an **assessment centre**. It is a term which can be confusing in that it applies to a **process** of gathering evidence about a candidate's suitability for a post, rather than the geographical location where the tests take place. In an assessment centre, candidates are put through a series of tests, simulations, exercises and interviews, specifically designed to measure their abilities against a checklist of competencies which are known to be relevant to the particular job. The basic idea is to collect as much information about a candidate using the widest range of evidence possible. Trained assessors then use that information to make judgements about each candidate's strengths and weaknesses in different areas.

An assessment centre can often take two or more days to complete and it may involve physical tests as well as group work, role play exercises, and psychological assessments. In an assessment centre candidates are observed at all times. Even when the formal tests are over and candidates are relaxing in the evening, company executives may be present to see who makes friends easily, who retreats behind a newspaper, and even who has one drink too many.

Within an assessment centre, the interview is seen as a part of a much wider selection process. Performance at interview is only one of a variety of measures used to enable a selection panel to make its decision.

### Interviewing for technical posts

Before the formal interview, you'll need to get a view of candidates' levels of technical skills applicable to the job. Some candidates may offer high level qualifications to support their applications, but a degree in chemistry, for example, probably suggests a general knowledge of the subject rather than an in-depth knowledge of any particular branch of the science. Bear in mind also, that the rate of progress and change is such that the practical value of a science degree is severely time-limited these days.

If, as a manager, you aren't fully aware of the technical aspects of the job you are recruiting to, ask your colleagues to devise a test to identify those candidates who have the appropriate knowledge, and those who would need training. In addition you could put candidates through more than one interview. Begin, for example, with a **technical interview** to ascertain the level of knowledge and expertise. This leaves you free to use a second interview to concentrate on other requirements of the job such as willingness to undertake training, ability to work alongside col-leagues, motivation *etc*. If two interviews are an impractical suggestion, then make sure that candidates are interviewed by a panel in which at least one member has the necessary technical knowledge to explore this aspect of the job for you.

## Interviewing for administrative posts

Work sample tests and simulations lend themselves easily to recruiting administrative staff. In instances where the job also requires a high level of contact with the public, it can be useful to ask a colleague to show each candidate around the premises, introducing them to staff as they go. First impressions count a lot with the public and so initial responses to each candidate from the staff can be useful indicators of their social skills. Some companies ask receptionists for their first impressions of candidates as they arrive for interview.

## Interviewing for manual jobs

Use tests to gain an insight into skills and potential. This leaves you free to use the interview to explore other areas with candidates, such as their previous experience, work records, health matters, and attitudes to work.

## PREPARING TO INTERVIEW

Many employers are more nervous of the interview than candidates. This is hardly surprising when you consider that:

- Many candidates will have had several recent interview experi-ences, whereas some employers may interview no more than two or three times within a five-year period.

- Candidates have everything to gain and little to lose, whereas a poor recruitment decision can cost the company and a manager dearly.

- Many candidates, even school leavers, will have had direct training in interview technique, whereas many managers have not had the benefit of recruitment training.

- Research suggests that untrained interviewers tend to gain a view of a candidate during the first four minutes of the interview. They then unwittingly spend the rest of the interview seeking to confirm their view of the candidate. In effect, the odds seem to be stacked against the interviewer. The research suggests that in an interview the candidate only has to *shine* for the first four minutes.

## Preparing the ground

Begin with the simple nuts and bolts:

● Agree an interview date and, if it is to be a panel interview, ensure other panel members have blocked a suitable period out of their diaries.

● Allocate approximately 30 minutes to each interview and an additional 20 or 25 minutes per candidate of you have asked candidates to make a presentation. Allow up to an hour after the interviews for discussion and decision-making.

● Print and distribute a simple interview schedule similar to the one illustrated in Figure 22. Make sure that all panel members and anyone else involved in the process, such as test organisers and receptionists, are given a copy. If there are more than four candidates to interview ensure that your schedule makes allowances for coffee and lunch breaks.

---

**CARIBBEAN TRAVEL SPECIALISTS**
**INTERVIEW SCHEDULE**
**Trainee Travel Manager (Kensington Branch)**

Interviews for the above post will take place on Monday 18th December at the Kensington Branch Office, Lower Heathgate St. The schedule is as follows:

|                  |   |          |
|------------------|---|----------|
| Andrew Phillips  | – | 1.00 pm  |
| Lorraine Haworth | – | 1.30 pm  |
| Tom Sugden       | – | 2.00 pm  |
| Ann Beverage     | – | 2.30 pm  |

Panel:

|               |   |                           |
|---------------|---|---------------------------|
| Ann Poole     | – | Branch Manager            |
| Clare Waters  | – | Area Manager              |
| Mark Swindon  | – | Personnel &               |
|               |   | Administration Manager    |

---

Fig. 22. Example of an interview schedule.

- Book the interview room and ensure that all necessary interview and test materials will be available on the day. You may also need to ensure that a separate room is available for work sample tests. Think also about what you intend to do with candidates after the interview. Will you send them home or keep them on the premises until you have made your choice? If you choose the latter, you'll need to arrange accommodation and refreshments.

- Make sure all applications and reference materials are copied to panel members well in advance of the interview. Arrange for the panel to meet at least half an hour before the first candidate arrives in order that members can agree their strategies for obtaining the information they need.

- Write a simple letter to shortlisted candidates inviting them to attend an interview. Figure 23 is a sample of such a letter. It can be adapted easily to suit most situations. Points to note are that it gives a time and location for the event, it asks candidates to undertake some work beforehand and it requires them to confirm their intention to attend.

### Filling the 30 minutes
If you are unused to interviewing, you may wonder how on earth you can fill the 30 minutes of an interview with meaningful questions and serious dialogue. More experienced interviewers however, will tell you that the real problem lies in obtaining all the information you need in so short a time.

## SETTING THE QUESTIONS

A good interview is a structured event. To be successful as an interviewer you must do your homework and ensure that there is method and a purpose to the questions you ask. Thanks to the job description and person specification which you wrote, you know what skills and qualities you are looking for. Now you must prepare your questions to make sure that you have all the information you need about a candidate before he leaves the room. No matter how tense and unnatural the experience may seem to you, your job is to ensure that the discussion progresses logically, covering all the requirements of the job.

### Asking open questions
There are two types of questions used at interview. Each has a specific

Headstart Programmes Plc
St Helier House
Western Way
Plymbourne
Essex
PL7 5PS

Tel: 01654 972358

15/10/9X

Dear Mr Harris

Thank you for your application for the post of Sales Manager in our town office.

I would be pleased if you could attend for interview at 2.30 pm on Tuesday 7th November at the above address.

In preparation for the interview please write a brief report outlining the steps you would take to create a successful sales team within a company such as ours. I should be grateful to receive a copy of your report for consideration by the interview panel no later than Tuesday 31st October .

Please telephone to confirm that you are able to attend interview.

Yours sincerely


Simon North
**Area Manager (South West)**

Fig. 23. Letter inviting a shortlisted candidate to attend an interview.

purpose. You can use them deliberately to obtain the information you need.

**Open questions** are used to encourage a candidate to talk about himself, his background and experience, and his feelings about the job he is applying for. The words of the question are purposely chosen to ensure that he cannot easily give a simple one word answer. Open questions often begin with phrases like:

- 'How do you feel about . . .?'.
- 'What do you think are the most. . .?'
- 'How do you see the development of . . .?'

Questions such as these enable a candidate to talk himself into or out of a job. They can create a relaxed, natural feel to an interview but you must pay careful attention to responses. Make sure candidates are really giving you an answer to your question rather than a repetition of a carefully rehearsed speech. Whenever you use open questions, try to ensure that you have a supplementary question up your sleeve, just in case you feel that the candidate is ducking the issue or missing your central point.

## Using closed questions

**Closed questions** are used to obtain hard information. They usually require short answers. A closed question often begins with 'Do you . . .?', and the usual response has to be 'Yes I do', or 'No I don't.' You can use closed questions either to check basic factual information or to press a candidate into making a firm statement if you feel that his responses to your open questions are too vague or woolly. Candidates faced with questions such as these have to come off the fence and answer appropriately.

## Preparing the questions

Preparation is the key to successful interviewing.

- Prepare your questions in advance.

- Ensure that the questions set by you and your colleagues cover every aspect of the job description and person specification.

- Look at candidates' applications and decide where the emphasis of the interview should lie for each individual. What information do you need to gain from this candidate in particular?

● Try to have a supplementary question ready for use in case your first question doesn't give you the quality of information you require.

● Use **open** and **closed** questions appropriately.

## INTERVIEWING

There are many ways to structure an interview. Here is a tried and tested example which works well.

1. Begin the interview with a simple icebreaker question designed to establish a relationship between you and the candidate. This initial question will set you both at ease. 'Tell me, Mr Robinson, what particularly attracts you to this line of work?' or 'Could you tell me briefly a little about yourself and why you have applied for this job?'

2. Then cluster your questions around the five-point or seven-point person specification headings mentioned in Chapter 2 on pages 34 and 39.

3. Clear up any outstanding issues and check basic facts.

4. Close the interview thanking the candidate for his attendance and asking if he has any questions for you or the panel.

### Clustering questions

When interviewing experienced candidates it can be extremely useful to structure each cluster of questions to move from theoretical questions to practical questions and back again. Ask questions about hypothetical situations and then request practical examples of how the candidate has dealt with similar situations in the past. Move from general questions, 'What would you do if . . .?, to specific ones, 'When did you last use a piece of machinery like this?', or 'What was the size of the budget you were responsible for in your last job?' Sound theoretical knowledge added to successful past experience counts for a lot.

Other supplementary questions can arise from candidates' responses. A simple challenge such as – 'Are you really saying that . . .?', can be very effective.

### Creating stress

Some jobs are highly stressful, in which case, it is legitimate to deliberately create a stressful situation in order to see how a candidate handles it. An interview however, is not an intellectual point-scoring exercise. Your role is to gain evidence about a candidate's suitability for a job, not to beat him into submission. Challenge statements he makes in order to gain a deeper understanding but don't challenge every general statement just for the sake of it.

## READING THE SIGNS

Human begins are complex sophisticated creatures operating at different levels simultaneously. We all send out messages by a variety of means and it is important that interviewers try to understand all that is happening during the interview process. In particular, pay as much attention to a candidate's body language as to his speech. Body language works almost at a subconscious level and it can tell you a great deal about a candidate. From your point of view this is most noticeable when a candidate's spoken words appear to be contradicted by his body language.

### Body language

For interview, most candidates are trained to sit slightly forward in their chairs with their hands on their laps. They know not to fidget. They are told this to ensure that the words they speak are supported by the messages their bodies are sending out. Occasionally however, you'll spot a chink in the armour and despite what the candidate is saying, his body language will be making a different more honest statement. At such times you'll have a feeling of unease and his statements won't ring true. No wonder most of us learn never to take anything at face value.

### Extreme examples
Watch out for:

- The candidate who wrings his hands and bites his nails as he tells you that he can handle stressful situations.

- The candidate who leans back in his chair and puts his hands behind his head as he tells you he is bright and alert.

- The candidate who avoids eye contact.

- The candidate who stares at the ceiling or towards the distant horizon as he runs movies in his head, struggling to find an answer that he hopes you would like to hear.

## HANDLING SENSITIVE INFORMATION

At times during the recruitment process you may have to ask questions of a sensitive nature. This can be difficult for both you and the candidate. It can be made easier however, if you make it clear that the information will not leave the room. Occasionally, a simple question, mopping up at the end of an interview, can lead you into a sensitive area. This can be particularly true for matters concerning health and criminal convictions.

### Getting a view of criminal convictions

The Rehabilitation of Offenders Act 1974 allows people with criminal records to have the slate wiped clean after a certain period. In many instances therefore, it is quite possible for a candidate who has been found guilty of a criminal offence to tell you that they do not have a criminal record. This period of time is called the rehabilitation period. Its length is dependent on the offence and the sentence given.

### Understanding the Rehabilitation of Offenders Act

People aged 17 or over when convicted, who are given a sentence of more than six months but less than two and a half years have a rehabilitation period of ten years. Those aged under 17 at the time of the conviction are given a five-year rehabilitation period. Those over 17 years of age given prison sentences of six months or less would have rehabilitation periods of seven years, and those under 17 years of age at the time of conviction would have to wait three and a half years before they could state that they had no criminal record. There are shorter rehabilitation periods for offences which incurred fines, community service orders, probation, supervision or care orders. The rehabilitation period is calculated from the date of conviction. After this period, in most cases, provided the sentence was not more than two and a half years, a candidate does not need to tell you about it even if he is asked.

Candidates with criminal records which are not yet spent, have to declare them only if they are asked. Many candidates are aware of this and may choose not to disclose their past record in the hope that you won't ask. Others however, will take steps to break the news to you in a private conversation beforehand, in a confidential letter, or in a statement returned to you along with the application form.

Of itself, a criminal record should not deter you from employing someone. Treat the disclosure as any other piece of evidence about a candidate and ask yourself:

- How long ago was the offence committed?

- Does the nature of the offence have any bearing on the job the candidate is applying for?

- Is the candidate's explanation plausible?

- Has sufficient time passed to suggest that the candidate's behaviour has changed?

Some people prefer not to disclose information until they are offered the job, so if a clean record is important to you, make sure you ask the question at interview or include a section requiring disclosure of information on the application form.

### Understanding the exceptions

There are some jobs to which the Rehabilitation of Offenders Act does not apply. In these instances candidates must declare all criminal convictions no matter how old they are. These include:

- Paid or voluntary jobs in which there is substantial access to people under the age of 18.

- Professions which have legal protection, such as lawyers, doctors, dentists, nurses and chemists.

- Jobs where national security may be at risk, such as some civil service posts, defence contractors, and sensitive jobs within the BBC, British Telecom or the Post Office.

### RECORDING YOUR FINDINGS

Even with only four or five people shortlisted, by the time you have interviewed the final candidate, you will have trouble recollecting the detail of earlier interviews. It is important therefore, to establish a system for recording your impressions of each candidate at the end of, if not during, each interview. In panel interviews, it is also important that all members are agreed about the particular mix of skill, experience and temperament they are looking for and that they too can individually record their thoughts about each candidate while the interview is still fresh in their minds.

**Global Systems Plc**
Scoresheet for Panel Member
Secretary to the Managing Director

| Candidate No. | 1 | 2 | 3 | 4 | 5 |
|---|---|---|---|---|---|

## Physical

Good general health
Presentable appearance
Well spoken – articulate

## Attainment

GCSE English
Maths
Good level of education
Further education
PC Competence

## Intelligence

Logical
Planning ability
Eye for detail

## Special aptitudes

Teamworker
People skills
Establishing office systems
Dealing with the public
Scheduling meetings
Taking minutes
Preparing agendas

## Interests

Current affairs
People

## Disposition

Outgoing
Discreet
Dependable
Assertive when necessary

## Circumstances

Occasional travel required

Fig. 24. A scoresheet for an interviewer, based on the five-point plan.

# Global Systems Plc
## Summary of panel findings
### Secretary to the Managing Director

| | Average score for Candidate No. 1 | 2 | 3 | 4 | 5 |
|---|---|---|---|---|---|
| **Physical** | | | | | |
| Good general health | | | | | |
| Presentable appearance | | | | | |
| Well spoken – articulate | | | | | |
| **Attainment** | | | | | |
| GCSE English | | | | | |
| Maths | | | | | |
| Good level of education | | | | | |
| Further education | | | | | |
| PC Competence | | | | | |
| **Intelligence** | | | | | |
| Logical | | | | | |
| Planning ability | | | | | |
| Eye for detail | | | | | |
| **Special aptitudes** | | | | | |
| Teamworker | | | | | |
| People skills | | | | | |
| Establishing office systems | | | | | |
| Dealing with the public | | | | | |
| Scheduling meetings | | | | | |
| Taking minutes | | | | | |
| Preparing agendas | | | | | |
| **Interests** | | | | | |
| Current affairs | | | | | |
| People | | | | | |
| **Disposition** | | | | | |
| Outgoing | | | | | |
| Discreet | | | | | |
| Dependable | | | | | |
| Assertive when necessary | | | | | |
| **Circumstances** | | | | | |
| Occasional travel required | | | | | |
| **Test results** | | | | | |
| Production of routine letter | | | | | |
| Bookkeeping reconciliation | | | | | |
| **Total scores** | | | | | |

Fig. 25. An example of a summation score sheet.

Once again the person specification can be the key to developing a simple scoresheet for interviewers. The scoresheet illustrated in Figure 24 was used in the recruitment of a secretary. It is based on the job specification and seven-point plan mentioned in Chapter 2. Rather than using vague headings such as **qualifications** and **specific skills** however, the actual qualifications and skills required are listed. Panel members will already have evidence of some skills and qualifications appropriate to the job from application forms and references. The scorecard allows them to confirm the validity of earlier evidence and to record their findings about the candidates as other evidence comes to light during the interview.

## EVALUATING THE EVIDENCE

Figure 25 is a summation scoresheet for an administrative assistant job. In the case of panel interviews, discussion and comparison of notes on each candidate will enable you to arrive at a consensus view based on information obtained at interview. Additional cells on the scoresheet also allow work sample test scores, responses from referees, and additional (valued added) skills to be taken account of in identifying the most appropriate candidate.

Often scoresheets such as these can clearly highlight the most appropriate candidate for a given job and panel members may be happy to accept the recommendation. The main purpose of the scoresheet however, is to promote discussion and add structure to the decision-making process when the relative merits of candidates are discussed at the end of the interview.

## MAKING YOUR CHOICE

Tests, references, letters of application, informal first impressions, and interview performance, may all add to your view of the suitability of a candidate for the job you have to offer. Scoresheets can often highlight the candidate who appears to have the strongest mix of ability and experience. Sometimes however, despite all the evidence, you may still feel unhappy with the scoresheet recommendation.

● Sometimes from a shortlist of five, you may discover that three candidates could fulfil all the duties of the job description, but each would do the job in a very different way.

● As a learning experience for all involved, the recruitment and selection process may alter your view of the job and so the score-sheet may fail to take account of aspects of the job which were initially considered to be unimportant.

● Frequently a candidate with relatively little experience will score poorly against a more experienced rival. The less experienced candidate however, could have a much better long-term potential and have a more appropriate temperament and personality. At such times, it is worth remembering that skills can often be developed through training, whereas personal characteristics are more difficult to develop and change.

### Risk taking

At the end of the day, despite attempts at objectivity, recruitment and selection is a human activity and occasionally you have to be prepared to take a risk. The biggest risk is to appoint someone who you feel may not be able to fulfil the requirements of the job. Strangely however, many managers appear happier to do this than to take a decision not to appoint at all.

### SUMMARY

● The job interview is part of a much wider process of gathering evidence of suitability for a job.

● Tests done before the formal interview can provide reliable evidence of a candidate's interest, aptitude or ability.

● Psychometric tests can be of use to you if you regularly appoint people to standard posts or if you need to recruit a large number of people for a new project.

● Work sample tests are the easiest to develop and administer. They can be created by devising a simple practical exercise based upon the realities of the job to be done.

● Interviews give you the chance to get to know the person behind the application form and see how his approach will fit in with that of your organisation. Different organisations have different methods and procedures. Some have no methods at all!

- The simplest selection interview is the one-to-one meeting between you and the candidate. When they work out well these interviews are the closest thing to a natural conversation. They can be pleasant relaxed affairs but they can go badly wrong.

- Panel interviews are popular because they reduce the possibility of personal idiosyncrasies affecting the decision.

- Sequential interviewing enables you to expose candidates to a wide range of interviewers who may use each interview to concentrate upon particular aspects of the job.

- The final stage of selecting a candidate should be a structured, evidence gathering, event.

- A good interview has to have structure. To be successful as an interviewer you must do your homework and ensure that there is a method and a purpose to the questions you ask.

- Pay as much attention to a candidate's body language as to his speech. Body language works almost at a subconscious level. It can tell you a great deal about a candidate.

- Establish a system for recording your impressions of each candidate at the end of, if not during each interview. The person specification can be the key to developing a simple scoresheet.

- Scoresheets promote discussion and add structure to the decision-making process when the relative merits of candidates are discussed at the end of the interview.

- At the end of the day however, despite attempts at objectivity, recruitment and selection remains a human activity and occasionally you have to be prepared to take a risk. The biggest risk is to appoint someone who may not be able to fulfil the requirements of the job. Be prepared *not* to make an appointment.

## CASE STUDIES

### John takes a sophisticated approach

In his search for an administrative assistant John decides to select his new member of staff on the basis of a panel interview supported by a few work sample tests. Devising the tests proves harder than he had imagined, largely because he discovers that he is not as familiar with the job to be filled as he initially thought. In retrospect he realises that this task could have been delegated to the person who is vacating the post. Because of the time wasted in developing the test, John discovers he doesn't have a great deal of time to spend with panel members preparing for the interview. Neither is he able to spend much time preparing his own questions. The situation deteriorates even further on the day of the interview when panel members discover that John, in his haste, has forgotten to book the interview room and has made no arrangements for the administration of the test he has devised. Arrangements are still being made as the first candidate arrives.

### Trish knows what she wants

Trish has a clear idea of the type of person she wants in this post and so she has no need for tests or interview panels. Her staff organise the interview schedule and book the appropriate rooms so that she can hold one-to-one interviews with the shortlisted candidates. Unfortunately, although she has a clear idea of what she is looking for, she hasn't considered what questions to ask in order to obtain the information she needs. As a result, the interviews prove to be difficult encounters and she struggles to keep the conversation going. Asking open rather than closed questions would have made the event more productive.

### Mark is driven by nervous energy

Recruiting the right staff is a central pillar of Mark's strategy to develop this company. He is nervous however. This is the first time he has been in charge of recruitment and he doesn't want to appear an idiot in the eyes of the candidates and his colleagues. He delegates the booking of the room and the scheduling arrangements to his staff and asks the outgoing member of staff to devise a couple of work sample tests which he can use with shortlisted candidates. Because of this lack of confidence at interview he also asks candidates to prepare a short presentation on how they would develop a particular aspect of the job. He then calls a brief meeting of the panel members and asks each member to take responsibility for one specific area of the interview. Then he writes out a cluster of questions for each characteristic of the job. The questions move from theoretical to practical and in the main they are open-ended. Finally, he lists the bare facts that he needs to check with each candidate and prepares closed questions to obtain the information he needs. Mark finds that the interview and tests go well – surprisingly at the end he discovers that his preparation was so thorough that he didn't need to refer to his notes at all.

## DISCUSSION POINTS

1. How important is this recruitment to the wellbeing of your company?

2. Which aspects of the process do you need to keep control of?

3. Which aspects can you delegate to others?

4. What systems are you going to establish to identify the most appropriate candidate?

# 5
# Bringing Your Candidate on Board

## MAKING AN INITIAL OFFER

It makes a great deal of sense, at the end of an interview, to ask each candidate if he would be still interested in taking the job if it were offered to him. It may seem like a crazy question but an interview is a two-way process, and by the end, both you and the candidate will be changed people! In particular, the interview process may have changed his view about working for your organisation, so on that basis your question is quite reasonable. To some extent however, the candidate's response to your question will be governed by his level of knowledge about the proposed salary and the terms and conditions of his employment.

If you have already stated the salary and the terms and conditions of employment, most candidates should be able to give you a straightforward answer to your question but candidates will be less able to give you a direct answer if the terms and conditions have not been explained or if the salary is 'negotiable'.

- When a candidate knows the salary and terms and conditions and he has confirmed his continued interest in the job, you can be fairly confident that he will accept the job if it is offered to him after the interview.

- If he doesn't know the salary and terms and conditions however, you may have to enter into some negotiation to secure his acceptance. In such instances, it is important to try to identify a 'second favourite' candidate and also to have a clear view of your limit with regard to salary and other terms and conditions.

### Making a verbal offer
It is almost certain that your initial offer will be made verbally shortly after the end of the interview, perhaps by telephone a few hours or days

later. Even though a candidate may accept your verbal offer however, it is unlikely that he will hand in his notice with his present employer until he gets something in writing from you.

### Limiting your offer

In making your offer of employment, make sure you inform the candidate of any conditions which limit your statement. At this stage, for example, your offer may be subject to:

- receipt of satisfactory references
- receipt of confirmation of qualifications
- a medical check.

## INFORMING OTHER CANDIDATES

Whenever possible, try to avoid informing other candidates of your decision until you have secured a verbal acceptance from your preferred candidate. Sometimes successful candidates change their minds about wanting the job on their way home, before you offer it to them. At such times, you may wish to offer a post to one of the other candidates who you interviewed. It is helpful if you are able to offer this candidate the job, without having previously told him that his application was unsuccessful.

Figures 26 and 27 are 'sorry' letters to candidates who have been unsuccessful after interview. As with other correspondence to applicants, there is a great deal to be gained by being polite and sympathetic. Letters such as the one illustrated in Figure 27 are particularly useful in situations where you would welcome another application from this candidate in the future.

## CHECKING DETAILS

While it is perfectly reasonable for successful candidates to be unwilling to hand in their notice until they have an offer from you in writing, there is a danger that critical resignation and appointment dates can be missed in the log jam. Teachers, for example, generally have to give a half-term's notice to their present employer before taking up a post elsewhere. Missing the crucial half-term resignation date can mean that the teacher must remain with his present employer for an additional six or seven weeks. This has an enormous impact upon the recruiting headteacher who then has to plan a strategy to take account of the fact that he will be one teacher short for the first half of the coming term.

## Awaiting references

If you have been moving swiftly through the recruitment process, you may have shortlisted, interviewed, and agreed on your preferred candidate before referees have had the chance to respond to your letter or questionnaire. At such times, you can make a written offer of employment which contains a statement making the offer 'subject to the receipt of satisfactory references'.

## Checking qualifications

How far back do you wish to go? Many employers are content to be furnished with proof of the attainment of the highest award or qualification claimed by a candidate. There would be little point in asking for proof of a candidate's attainment of GCSE history for example, if he could produce his Business Studies degree certificate.

Sometimes however, it is important to obtain proof of specific qualifications required for the job. A canoe instructor, a lifeguard, or a swimming instructor, should all be able to produce evidence of their training and current competence in these activities.

## Checking health

Not so long ago, many local authorities used to require all successful job candidates to undergo medical checks prior to employment. These days, many have revised that policy in the light of evidence from insurance companies which suggests that it is a fairly safe bet to employ administrative staff under 40 years old without requiring a medical check. The statistics showed that it was more expensive to run a medical check for every member of staff under 40, than it was to pay out for those one or two members of staff from that age group who became ill during their employment.

However, while this may be fine for sedentary administrative posts, some other jobs may require a more rigorous consideration of health matters. In general, the nature of the job determines the level of physical health and fitness required. As with references and qualifications therefore, you may decide to make your written offer of employment subject to a satisfactory health check by a doctor.

## Minimising delays

None of the above should cause delays to the signing of the employment agreement and the determination of a start date for your new employee.

**Motto Recruitment Services
Highlands House
Pearce Way
Leeds 6
LD56 7WY
Tel: 01347 884324**

12/3/9X

Dear Mr Holmes

Thank you for attending the interview for the post of
Recruitment Assistant. I enjoyed meeting you and hearing how
your career has developed to date and of your aspirations for the
future.

Unfortunately, having given a great deal of thought to all the
applications, I regret to advise you that one of the other
candidates more closely matches our requirements at this time.

I do hope that you will soon be successful in your search for a
new position.

Yours sincerely

Mrs S Walker
**Managing Director**

Fig. 26. An example of a letter to a candidate who has
been unsuccessful after interview.

12/3/9X

Dear Mr Holmes

Thank you for attending the interview for the Recruitment Assistant post recently. I enjoyed meeting you and hearing how your career has developed to date and of your aspirations for the future.

Unfortunately, having given a great deal of thought to all the applications, I regret to advise you that one of the other candidates more closely matches our requirements at this time.

I would like you to know however, that you had a very good interview and I hope this decision will not deter you from applying for any future vacancy which interests you.

Yours sincerely

Mrs S Walker
**Managing Director**

Fig. 27. An example of a letter to an unsuccessful candidate, but which encourages future applications.

On receipt of your written offer of employment, the successful candidate should have no problem in giving his present employer notice of his intention to leave. Despite the limitations of your offer, he should be reasonably confident of obtaining satisfactory references and he should know where he can lay his hands on evidence of his qualifications.

Understandably, older candidates may be a little apprehensive of undergoing a medical check, but you can point out that this is a simple, general procedure which is unlikely to throw up anything which he isn't already aware of. Many people have annual health checks and they pay a great deal of money for the privilege.

## UNDERSTANDING THE LEGAL REQUIREMENTS

In law, you should give every new employee a written statement of the main terms and conditions of his employment. This may be written in a letter of appointment or given in the form of a **contract**. Many employers send it out within a few days of offering a candidate the job but, if for any reason it is delayed, you must make sure that your new employee receives it within 13 weeks of starting work for you. Figure 28 shows you how to set out a written statement of employment which meets the requirements of sections 1–6 of the Employment Protection (Consolidation) Act 1978, as amended by the Trade Union Reform and Employment Rights Act 1993. Further details of legislation concerning written statements of employment are available from the employment department and ACAS (see useful addresses).

### Employment statements

Many letters or contracts contain much detail. In law however, there is a basic minimum amount of information which an employee must be given:

● The name of the employer, the employee and the title of the job.

● The rate of pay and pay arrangements (weekly or monthly for example).

● Details of the normal working hours.

● Holiday arrangements (including bank holiday arrangements).

● Arrangements for incapacity to work due to sickness or injury, including sick pay and pension arrangements.

● The entitlement of an employer and employee to notice of termination or, in the case of a non-permanent employment, the period for which employment is expected to continue, or the termination date of a fixed-term contract.

● Details of the location of the place of work.

● Details of collective agreements, disciplinary and grievance procedures.

*Adding detail*
More sophisticated contracts may also include details of any probationary period which your new employee is required to work. Are you happy to offer a permanent contract immediately or would you prefer to confirm the appointment after a period of, say, six months?

## Producing a statement of employment
Figure 28 illustrates the layout of a typical statement of the terms of employment. It takes account of the basic legal requirements and other details mentioned above.

## Contracting part-time staff
Employees working part-time have the same statutory employment rights as those working full-time. Under recent legislation, part-time workers qualify for employment rights on exactly the same basis as full-time workers. Like full-time workers, part-timers now have to complete only two years continuous service with their employer before they qualify, regardless of the number of hours they work each week.

In effect, part-time staff have the same statutory rights as those working full-time with regard to sex and race discrimination, unlawful deductions from salary, time off for anti-natal care, and the right to time off for trade union duties and activities. On completion of the two year period they also qualify for unfair dismissal and redundancy payment rights.

## BUILDING ON STRENGTHS

When the process is finished and the contract is signed, you will have a great deal of information about the successful candidate. For example, you will know:

● the level of his technical knowledge

# Written Statement of Employment

1.  You (**name of employee**) began employment with (**name of employer**) on (**Date employment started or will start**).

2.  Your previous employment with (**name of company**) does (**or does not**) count as part of your period of continuous employment.

3.  You are employed as (**either give a job title, or a brief description of the work**).

4.  Your place of work is (**location of workplace or places**) and the address of your employer is (**address of employer**).

5.  You pay will be (**give particulars of scale or rate of renumeration, or the method of calculating renumeration**).

6.  You will be paid (**give particulars of the intervals at which renumeration is to be paid**).

7.  Your hours of work are (**give particulars including details of normal working hours**).

8.  Your holiday entitlement is (**give enough information to enable an employee to calculate entitlement, including accrued holiday pay on termination**).

9.  In case of incapacity for work, (**give the terms and conditions relating to sickness or injury and any provision for sick pay**).

10. Particulars of pensions and pension schemes are (**either give particulars or refer to other documents**).

11. The amount of notice of termination of your employment you are entitled to receive is (**give period of notice**).

12. The amount of notice you are required to give is (**either state the amount or refer to relevant legislation or other documents**).

13. Your employment is (**state whether the employment is:**
    (a) **permanent, subject to the terms described in 11, above**
    (b) **fixed term – give termination date**
    (c) **temporary – give period of likely duration.**

Fig. 28. Example of a written statement of employment.

114

14. The collective agreements which directly affect the terms and conditions of your employment are (**give information about relevant agreements**).

15. The disciplinary rules which apply to you are (**give an explanation of the rules**). They can be found in (**refer to other documents**).

16. If you are dissatisfied with any disciplinary decision which affects you, you should apply to (**explain how applications should be made**).

17. If you have a grievance about your employment you should make your application to (**explain how grievances are to be raised, the steps involved and where further information is located**).

18. A contracting out certificate under the Social Security Pensions Act 1975 is/is not in force for the employment this statement is being issued for (**delete as appropriate**).

Statements for employees normally employed in the UK but required to work abroad for the same employer for a period of more than one month should also cover the **period** for which employment abroad is to last, the **currency** in which the employee is to be paid, any **additional benefits** and **terms** relating to the employees' return to the UK.

*Note 1*: You must ensure that when referring to other documents, your employees have reasonable opportunities to read those documents in the course of their employment or that they are given reasonable access to them in some other way.

*Note 2*: An employer with fewer than 20 employees (including the employee who will be issued with the statement) need not include the information specified in paragraphs 15 and 16. With regard to grievance procedures mentioned in paragraph 17, it is sufficient for such an employer to simply mention who within the company the matter should be taken to.

Fig. 28. Continued.

- his particular strengths
- aspects of his expertise which are currently not within your organisation
- areas of weakness or lack of experience
- his interview skills.

You may also have been able to gain a general impression of his career goals and his potential for further development within the company.

While your information is up-to-date and while your new member of staff is highly motivated by the prospect of a new and exciting job, now is the time to invite him to come and talk to you about his entry into your organisation.

### Holding an initial meeting

Clearly this meeting with your new employee should be much less formal than your previous encounter. Now is the time to relax a little and let him know that you are genuinely pleased to welcome him aboard. There is much to be gained at this meeting however, and so although it is informal, it should not be without structure.

- Begin your discussion by highlighting aspects of his application and interview which were particularly strong. Congratulate your new employee on his performance, and then discuss how best you can use his skills or experience in those areas. Even if your company's methods or systems are slightly different from those he is used to, you can indicate the need to get up to speed in these aspects of the job fairly quickly.

- Point out areas of the job which may be unfamiliar, and discuss how best to acquire the skills needed. Maybe you'll decide to put him working alongside a more experienced member of staff for a while, or maybe he'll opt to undertake a training course. He may have ideas of his own to contribute.

- Talk to him also about where he'll be working and tell him a little about the people he'll be working with. At this stage he'll be eager to make a good impression and he'll take on board what you say.

- Suggest some ways to prepare, between now and the start date. There may be a few books, articles, or company reports to read, some training possibilities to explore, or he may wish to familiarise himself with the neighbourhood and the community you serve, or maybe it would be beneficial for him to make contact with one or two of your colleagues, other members of your staff, or key clients.

- Finally, at the end of the meeting make sure your new employee has a clear understanding of the start date and time, where to go on his first day, and to whom he should report.

### Understanding the purpose

Beyond congratulations and a simple word of welcome to the company, the purpose of the meeting is to:

- lay the foundation for a good working relationship
- smooth the entry of your new member of staff into your organisation
- obtain maximum benefit from his current energy and motivation
- impress on the new employee that you have high expectations, and that you will be taking a keen supportive interest in his performance.

### SUMMARY

- At the end of the interview make a point of asking each candidate if they are still interested in taking the job.

- Even though a candidate may accept your verbal offer, it is unlikely that he will hand in his notice with his present employer until he gets something in writing from you.

- When making your offer of employment make sure you inform the candidate of any conditions which limit your offer. These limitations should not cause delays to the signing of the employment agreement and the determination of a start date for your new employee.

- Try to avoid informing other candidates of your decision until you have secured a verbal acceptance from your preferred candidate.

- In law, you should give every new employee a statement of the main terms and conditions of his employment. This is often written in a letter of appointment or given in the form of a contract.

- Contracts of employment are usually sent out within a few days of offering a candidate the job but, if for any reason it is delayed, you must make sure that your new employee receives it within 13 weeks of him starting work for you.

- While your information is up-to-date and while your new member of staff is highly motivated by the prospect of a new and exciting job, now is the time to invite him to come and talk to you about his entry into your organisation. This meeting should be much less formal than previous meetings.

- At the end of the meeting make sure your new employee has a clear understanding of the start date and time, where to go on the first day, and to whom to report.

## CASE STUDIES

### John misses the target

John's lack of planning made the selection process somewhat difficult. The interview schedule ran well over time and, as a result, the panel decided to reconvene the following day in order to make its decision. Some of the candidates on the day had also been disappointed by the lack of organisation and they began to question whether they really wanted to work for such a chaotic company. Later in the week, when John eventually makes contact with the preferred candidate to offer him the job, he is saddened to discover that the candidate has decided to decline the offer. 'I'm sorry,' he tells John, 'If you'd asked me at the end of the interview I would have told you then.'

### Trish makes her offer

The interview process hasn't been good for Trish either. Her lack of preparation means that she hadn't really got to know the candidates before the end of the interview. As the last candidate left she wondered how on earth she could decide between them. One candidate however stuck in her mind. He had worn a very distinctive tie and had seemed particularly eager to secure the job. 'He'll do,' she thought 'At least he's keen.'

When she telephoned the candidate he had no hesitation in accepting the post and so Trish arranged for a contract to be sent to him immediately. The contract was signed and returned to Trish the following day. It landed on her desk two days before his references arrived. They were the most appalling references she had ever seen.

## Mark faces a dilemma

Thanks to his careful preparation the interviews went well for Mark and the panel encountered no problems in identifying two candidates who could fulfil all the duties of the vacant post. Both candidates indicated that they were prepared to accept the post if it were offered to them, and both understood that any offer made would be subject to the receipt of satisfactory references.

Eventually, the panel made its choice between the candidates on the grounds that one had a language skill which could prove useful to the company within the next year or so.

## DISCUSSION POINTS

1.  What conditions will you place on your offer of employment?

2.  How do you intend to inform your successful candidate?

3.  What topics will you want to discuss with your new employee at the first meeting after you have offered him the job?

# 6
# Using Recruitment to Move Ahead

Recruiting the right staff is the key to developing your company, providing of course, you make the best use of the skills and attitudes they bring, and you take time to ensure that their energy and motivation is directed towards furthering the goals of your organisation in a structured, cohesive way. In some instances this may require a change in the 'culture' of your organisation. Answer the following questions:

1.  Do you have clear expectations of your staff?

2.  Do you know how to measure the success of your staff?

3.  Are the goals you set, related to the overall aims of your organisation?

4.  Do you involve your staff in setting goals and targets?

5.  Do you let your staff know that you value their thoughts and contributions?

6.  Do you ask questions, and take account of the ideas of others?

7.  Do you find solutions to problems through discussion with staff?

8.  Do you look for ways to help your staff achieve their goals?

9.  Do you spend more time acknowledging success rather than looking for faults?

10. Do you publicly acknowledge your staff's successes and achievements?

If you can answer 'yes' to most of these questions you are well on the way towards creating a climate within your company which will enable you to make the best use of your new employee.

## RELEASING POTENTIAL

A new member of staff has much more **potential** than a new machine. He will have a background of experience and will soon develop an intimate knowledge of the tasks you have set. If you have recruited well *your* new employee will be bright, alert and well-motivated. In effect, a new member of staff brings valuable ideas to an organisation and, given the right environment, will continue to develop these ideas as his knowledge increases. As a manager, your task is to release and channel the potential of every member of your team towards achieving the goals and targets of your organisation.

Good ideas are indiscriminate, they don't care where they land, so you must ensure that your staff's good ideas can find their way to your desk. Creating the right climate is the first step, but this alone isn't sufficient. Just as a machine needs careful installation, and scheduled regular servicing to ensure its continued performance, so you need to ensure that your new employee receives a structured induction into the organisation, and that afterwards you have a mechanism in place to enable him to take part in regular discussions regarding goals and performance.

## SETTING UP AN INDUCTION PROGRAMME

A new employee won't achieve maximum performance on the first day at work with you. The time it takes to get up to speed will depend on a number of factors, such as the nature and complexity of the job, and the level of training required. You've already invested a great deal of time in ensuring that you have recruited the right member of staff but now you must invest more time into making sure that he can begin to fulfil the promise he showed at interview. Use the interval of time between acceptance of the job and the start date to create an **induction programme** for your new employee.

The elements which make up an induction programme will vary according to the organisation and the nature of the job. In general however, an induction programme might include the following:

1.  **Getting to know the company**:
    Purpose of the organisation – mission statement and values.
    Relationship within the organisation – branch offices, franchises *etc*.

Who's who in the organisation.
Meeting the managing director and senior staff.
Tour of the organisation to meet colleagues and gain a view of the geography of the building.
Meeting with a selection of clients and suppliers.
Visits to customers.
Shadowing colleagues.
Invitations to take part in company social activities.

2. **Health and safety**:
Fire precautions and evacuation procedures.
First aid/medical facilities; what to do in the event of an accident; systems for reporting and recording accidents.
Particular health and safety warnings and procedures arising from the nature of the work to be undertaken by the employee, or due to the nature of processes or products used within the organisation.

3. **Security**:
Arrangements for access to the building.
Identification procedures.
Areas not open to the public.
Safeguarding computer systems.
Signing in and out.
Protection of buildings, vehicles and equipment.
Confidentiality.

4. **Training**:
Arrangements for training in the technical aspects of the job.
Company attitude to training and opportunities available.

5. **Employer/employee relationships:**
Confirmation of basic terms and conditions of employment, bonus schemes, overtime working, flexitime arrangements *etc.*
Pension options.
Holiday entitlement and procedures for booking leave.
Disciplinary and grievance procedures.
Union representatives.
Company policies regarding – customer care, use of telephone, change of employee addresses, overtime working *etc.*
Company arrangements for performance review and appraisal.

6. **Company expectations**:
Appearance.
Attitude.
How people address colleagues and customers.
Smoking policy.
Attitudes to alcohol.

Clearly, you cannot expect a new employee to assimilate so much information in one day. The best induction systems deliver the required information in 'bite-sized' pieces over an appropriate period of time. Often, if a new employee is also involved in learning technical aspects of the job, it can be very useful to break the monotony by mixing aspects of **general induction** with **technical training**.

### Making a beginning

With so much information to impart where do you begin? A useful starting point is to list the items which you feel he should know from the first day of his employment. Most new employees have two major fears:

● that they may not be able to fulfil the requirements of the job
● that they won't get on with their colleagues.

So it is essential therefore, that during the first day, your new employee successfully completes an aspect of the job he has been employed to undertake and that his immediate colleagues welcome him aboard.

Bear in mind also that he may be quite anxious and that first impressions can have a lasting impact. Few things are more off-putting to a new employee than to discover that no arrangements have been made for his arrival. Make sure, for example, that a desk or locker has been allocated to him and that any of the last incumbent's cast-offs have been cleared out.

If he is new to the company, he will require even the most basic everyday information. The following checklist could form the basis of a first day induction programme:

● repetition of contractual arrangements regarding hours of work
● carparking arrangements
● location of the employee's workstation or office
● breaks for refreshments
● lunch-break timing and facilities
● meeting immediate colleagues

- names of senior managers, roles, and how they should be addressed
- geography of the building
- location of cloakrooms and toilets
- staff noticeboards
- clocking in and out procedures
- fire procedures
- basic health and safety warnings
- what to do and who to see if he has a problem.

Don't overload him with information but make sure that he is able to get through his first day safely and that, by the end, he is aware that an induction programme has been established for him, and that he has a copy of the schedule to refer to.

### Thinking about timescales

An induction period which is too short will probably overwhelm a new employee with information. Too long an induction period however, will create frustration. Most employees are eager to be accepted into their new organisation and will not welcome an induction period stretching beyond one month. In many instances, the employee's own informal learning system will overtake a lengthy induction process, so make sure to arrange regular meetings with him to discuss progress in the job and in the induction programme. Most employees will tell you when they feel that the knowledge they have gained has outstripped the need for aspects of the planned induction.

### Ending induction

Let your new employee know when you consider the induction process to have ended. In general people thrive on achievement and the attainment of goals. The successful completion of an induction schedule is a significant milestone which should be acknowledged and celebrated.

Although induction may be over, you may still be waiting for your new employee to get up to speed on the technical or operational side of the job. The induction process may have also highlighted some aspects of the job for which further training is required, so use the **end of induction meeting** to begin a discussion about realistic targets, and timescales which both you and your new employee can agree.

### MAXIMISING PERFORMANCE

Companies which consistently get the best from their staff are those which manage to find solutions to two important questions:

1.  How do we ensure our employee achieves his maximum potential in the job?

2.  How do we keep his energies directed towards the targets set by the organisation?

Close attention to establishing an open and energetic culture, which recognises and rewards success, can go a long way towards achieving the first of these aims. However, a strong sense of direction is also vital, in order that the commitment and motivation of individual members of staff is translated into a common effort to achieve organisational goals. Staff energy may be dissipated by projects and the pursuit of targets which are, at best, peripheral to the main aims of the company.

**Business planning** and **performance review and appraisal** are two management processes which contribute towards determining a company's goals and ensuring that the workforce remains committed to achieving them. Both processes rely upon the active involvement of staff.

## Playing rugby?

In preparing for a match, the manager and coach of a rugby team will set a target. The target may be to win, to avoid losing, or to avoid a humiliating defeat. With an established target, team members will then probably contribute to the discussion about the best strategy to achieve the target. At the start of play, every team member will know what the team is trying to achieve, how they intend to achieve it, and what their team mates expect of them. In effect, they understand the team goal, and the importance of their individual role in the attainment of their team's ambition.

During the first half of the game, the role of the captain is very much one of encouraging, cajoling, and organising his team to meet developing situations as they occur. At half-time, as the players sit down and suck their oranges, they consider how well they have done. Are they achieving what they set out to do? Is the strategy working or do they need to make changes? They then decide on a strategy for the rest of the game and go back onto the field, with their captain playing a similar role once more. At the end of the match, the players review their performance, take on board any lessons learned, and then the process of planning for the next match begins again.

## BUSINESS PLANNING

You can draw an analogy between a rugby season and a period of a company's history. Let's imagine that the season equates to a one-year period of company activity. As with the match, the general aim of the organisation for that period should be simple and clear, to sell lightbulbs, produce cars, transport goods, train people and so on.

As with the rugby team however, particular strategies or game plans will have to be established within the general aims, in order to cope with the various challenges which the company will face over the coming year. Your role here, is to weigh up the opportunities and threats posed by competitors, partners, the business environment or technological development, and then to engage staff in deciding how best to meet these challenges and make the most of the opportunities.

This process of involving staff in strategic planning and goal setting is a very powerful management tool. If done correctly it enables all staff to:

- contribute to the development of the organisation
- realise the importance of the contribution made by them as individuals and members of the team.

In effect, each member of your staff becomes like a rugby player in the team. He knows what you are trying to achieve and he has taken part in determining how the team will go about it. In larger companies each section or department has its game plan and all members of staff can see how their contribution supports the overall company effort.

One result of the business planning process within a company is the publication of a business plan. In some companies these are glossy documents which are produced as much for the benefit of shareholders and investors as for staff. In such cases, it is easy for a manager to give more value to the published business plan, than to the process of dialogue and consultation which led to its production. In some instances, a senior manager may find it easier to invest a day of his time in producing a glossy vision of the future, than to go through the necessary consultation process with staff. Such plans however, are highly personalised and idiosyncratic. They might well convince shareholders and investors, but as a vehicle for uniting staff as a team with common aims and objectives, they are non-starters.

### Putting the process first

From your point of view the **process** of consultation and dialogue is the central mechanism for motivating staff and making the most of a company's human resources. In effect business planning works well if people are allowed to contribute their thoughts and ideas.

## USING PERFORMANCE REVIEW AND APPRAISAL

Once you have a clear sense of direction and a staff team who know where they are going and what is expected of them, you can use **performance review** and **appraisal** to link individual performance to the aims of the organisation.

Whereas business planning is about creating a team effort to achieve common goals, performance review and appraisal tends to concentrate on individual performance within the team. Your employee should view the process as a supportive mechanism which provides him with regular opportunities to step back from his day-to-day activities so that he can spend some time talking with you and thinking about:

- what he is doing and his contribution to the overall plan
- how well he is doing it
- what needs to be done in the future
- how best to ensure that future success is achieved.

### Getting down to essentials

Performance review and appraisal comprises regular one-to-one meetings between you and your employee. In some organisations such meetings take place every three months. Other organisations find a six-monthly or annual meeting is more appropriate. Some companies consider discussions about performance review to be different to appraisal interviews. Others make no distinction between the terms.

Those that do make a distinction usually argue that **performance review** is concerned with all the factors which can influence *performance* within a job, such as the working environment, the availability of materials and support, the speed of decision-taking, the quality of equipment *etc*. **Appraisal** however, is more concerned with the jobholder, his motivation and attitude, his skill and willingness to use his experience to solve problems, his potential for promotion and his needs for further training. Organisations which make such a distinction frequently devote the majority of meetings to performance review, keeping one meeting per year aside for an appraisal discussion.

Performance reviews and appraisal benefit the employee, the manager and the organisation in different ways.

*The employee*
A performance review and appraisal meeting with you should enable
your employee to:

● receive feedback on his contribution to the organisation's goals and
   targets
● gain recognition for his competence and capability
● develop increased autonomy within his job
● enhance his performance
● reduce wasted effort and activity
● reduce stress
● work to his strengths
● influence the work and how it is done.

*The manager*
For you, the manager, the meeting should enable you to:

● focus your employee's activity more precisely on priorities
● develop performance to meet changes in the environment
● set tasks to take account of developing capabilities
● improve relationships
● identify training needs.

*The organisation*
Performance review and appraisal should enable the organisation to:

● increase responsiveness to change
● improve the service to clients and customers
● reduce costs
● improve consistency of performance
● increase motivation.

## Reaching a common understanding
To work well, you will need to develop a common understanding
between you and your employee about the job: the priorities, and the difficulties which both of you face. For a new employee recruited to fulfil
the requirements of a new job description, there shouldn't be too many
problems here. It pays however, to revisit the situation from time to time.

## Preparing for a performance review and appraisal meeting
Performance review meetings should take place at regular intervals and

both you and your employee should know well in advance the date and time of the next meeting. As in all things, **preparation is the key to success**. Before you meet your employee to discuss performance, spend some time thinking about:

- the overall purpose of his job
- his main duties
- the performance standards you require
- targets and timescales which you agreed at the last meeting or in your meeting with him at the end of his induction programme
- results achieved and standards achieved
- problem areas
- future priorities in terms of his own performance and organisational requirements in the light of the business plan
- resource implications of the above
- his training and/or development needs.

### Helping your employee to prepare

Your employee should also be well prepared when he arrives to discuss his performance with you. You can help by making sure that he has sufficient notice of the meeting, that he fully understands the nature and range of the discussion and its purpose. Your employee should also be aware that you intend it to be a mutually beneficial meeting, so he should not view it as a threatening event. You may find it helpful to ask your employee to complete a short questionnaire such as the one in Figure 29. Point out to him, that you don't need to see the completed copy but that he may find it useful to refer to it during the meeting with you.

### Setting the tone

Try to arrange for the meeting to take place in a location where neither of you will be disturbed for at least an hour. If it must take place in your office, divert the telephone and let your colleagues know that you must not be disturbed. If you are asking your employee to comment upon his past and future performance within your organisation, it is only fair that you give him your uninterrupted attention.

Make the meeting appear informal. Sit alongside your employee rather than stare at him across the desk. Remember also that a major objective of the meeting is to work *with* him to determine future action. Effective teamwork arises from different people bringing different skills and experiences to bear on situations. Your employee's approach to the

**Preparing for a Performance Review and Appraisal Meeting**

Guidelines for Staff

> Performance Review and Appraisal meetings are one to one meetings between you and your manager. They are an opportunity for both of you to sit down quietly and discuss how well the work is going and to raise any matters which are of concern.

Performance Review

> This is the process of looking at the work you do and how it is affected by the way the work is organised, the equipment you use, the environment in which you work and the day to day problems you encounter.

Appraisal

> This is about how your skills, experience and personal attributes contribute to the way you perform in your job.

Preparation

> You can prepare for these meetings with your manager by making notes on the following topics. Keep these notes and take them with you when you go into the discussion. They may help you to remember what you want to say. Any notes you make are yours. They are confidential. You don't have to show them to anyone.
>
> What aspects of the job do you enjoy most/least?
>
> Has your performance changed since the last meeting with your manager?
>
> What are the main problems you encounter in carrying out your job?
>
> What do you think are your main skills?
>
> Are there any aspects of the job in which you lack confidence or would like more training?
>
> Do you have any ideas about how you could be more effective or make a greater contribution to the work?

Fig. 29. A questionnaire to help prepare for a performance review and appraisal meeting.

job and the problems which may arise, may be very different but nevertheless, just as effective as your own. Performance review is about **enabling your staff to become more effective** – not necessarily more like you.

## Holding the meeting

Your role in a performance review and appraisal meeting is to steer the discussion, summarise the main points, and agree the actions to be taken arising from what is said. To do this effectively, you will need to listen to what your employee has to say about his job, and the environment in which he works. As an active, interested listener you will also occasionally need to ask more searching questions in order to gain greater insight into what he is saying. Throughout the discussion, try to help your employee to take increasing responsibility for his own actions and performance. You can do this by encouraging him to put forward his facts and ideas first. Self-criticism and ideas for self-development and improvement are always more valuable than anything which you have to impose upon someone.

In the meeting try to strike a realistic balance between praise and criticism. Your employee cannot be expected to improve his performance if he is unaware of his strengths, but it is also important that he knows of areas where you feel improvements can be made. Avoid being negative however, when commenting on lack of achievement. Use constructive comments to highlight areas for improvement. In your discussion, be prepared to acknowledge your own mistakes or lack of direction or support, and be prepared to change your ideas if necessary.

## Closing and recording your meeting

At the end of the meeting summarise and write down what both you and your employee have agreed. **Remember, the object of the meeting is to improve performance by tying in your employee's energy and ideas to the aims of the organisation**. You'll probably find that the meeting results in a list of follow-up actions to be taken by both of you. From your point of view, try to avoid giving any undertakings, if there is any doubt in your mind about your ability to fulfil them. Be particularly careful about making promises which may depend upon the support of other people.

## Following up performance review and appraisal

Performance review and appraisal is expensive of time. A one-hour meeting twice a year for ten employees can take up 20 hours per year from your schedule. If you add a minimum of a further half-hour per employee/per year for your preparation and follow-up work, you'll find that you have invested 25 hours per year in the performance review and appraisal of your staff. If you consider their time as well as your own, then in the above example, your company investment in performance review and appraisal adds up to a minimum of 50 hours per year. As a manager you'll need to justify such an investment. There are two golden rules here:

1.  Make sure that the goals and targets which you agree with your employees are measurable. It isn't enough, simply to agree an area for improvement. You must establish a mechanism for identifying the improved performance. This can be done by:

    *stating a simple numerical measure – eg*:
    reduce the number of breakages by 10 per cent or
    increase production by 3 per cent.

    *stating a financial measure – eg*:
    reduce transport costs by 5 per cent in the next quarter.
    increase income from lettings by 5 per cent next year.

    *stating a timetable for achievement – eg*:
    produce a new sales brochure by March.
    introduce new accounting software by June.

2.  As with business planning, meetings are the easy part of the process. The difference between a successful scheme and one which rapidly becomes discredited is related to the amount of energy a manager puts into following up the agreements made between himself and his employees between meetings.

In effect, all things in business are interrelated. A company which concentrates upon sound recruitment strategies will not maximise its achievement without ensuring that a system is in place to make the best use of the staff it has recruited. A company which concentrates upon the skill, experience and motivation of its staff will not excel if it pays little attention to recruitment.

It is a well known fact that human drive and creativity has replaced coal, iron and steel as the raw material of the late twentieth century. The days when industry required high volume mindless labour are gone. Perhaps such days never really existed anyway. Today however, the future success of any organisation will depend upon the capability of its people. Quality people and quality management will give you the competitive edge and a place in the sunshine. Building such an organisation begins with recruiting the right staff. The solution lies with you. Do you want to join the premier league?

## SUMMARY

- Recruiting the right staff is the key to developing your company, providing you have a framework in place which directs them towards achieving the goals of your organisation.

- A new member of staff has much more potential than a new machine. He will have a background of experience and will soon develop an intimate knowledge of the tasks you have set him. If you have recruited well he will start out bright, alert and well-motivated.

- Part of that framework should include a structured induction into the organisation and a mechanism to enable him to take part in regular discussions about his goals and performance.

- Use the interval of time between acceptance of the job and the start date to create an induction programme for your new employee.

- The best induction systems deliver the required information in 'bite-sized' pieces over an appropriate period of time. Often, if a new employee is also involved in learning technical aspects of the job, it can be very useful to break the monotony by mixing aspects of 'general induction' with technical training.

- An induction period which is too short will probably overwhelm a new employee with information. Too long an induction period however, will create frustration.

- Let your new employee know when you consider the induction process to have ended. People thrive on achievement and the attainment of goals. The successful completion of induction is a landmark which should be recognised.

- Companies which get the best from their staff are those which ensure employees achieve their maximum potential and keep staff energies directed towards the targets set by the organisation.

- Without a strong sense of direction the commitment and motivation of individual members of staff may not translate into a common effort to achieve organisational goals.

- **Business planning** and **performance review and appraisal** are two management processes which contribute towards determining a company's goals and ensuring that the workforce remains committed to achieving them.

- Both mechanisms work well if people are allowed to contribute their thoughts and ideas.

- Business planning is about creating a team effort to achieve common goals. Performance review and appraisal concentrates on individual performance within the team through regular one-to-one meetings between you and your employee.

- Performance review meetings should take place in a location where neither of you will be distributed for at least an hour. If you must use your office, divert the telephone and let your colleagues know that you must not be disturbed.

- Your role in a performance review and appraisal meeting is to steer the discussion, summarise the main points, and agree the actions to be taken arising from what is said.

- Summarise what both you and your employee have agreed. You'll probably find that the meeting results in a list of follow-up actions to be taken by both of you. Do not make promises which you cannot keep.

- In business planning and performance review and appraisal, make sure that the goals and targets which you set with your employees are measurable.

- The difference between a successful business planning and performance review system, and one which becomes rapidly discredited is related to the amount of energy a manager puts into following-up the agreements made between himself and his employees in the interval between meetings.

● When it comes to recruiting the right staff, and getting the most out of them, the answer lies with you. Do you want to join the premier league?

## CASE STUDIES

### John's enthusiasm is overwhelming

Despite the setbacks John is determined that his new member of staff, his second choice, should get off to a good start and that he should be supported by a scheme of regular performance review and appraisal. The system he establishes is quite complicated and many of his existing staff have reservations about how effective it could be. Given John's track record there is a general fear that he will not respect confidentiality and that the scheme will fall into disuse the minute another management 'fad' takes his fancy. John however, takes the new member of staff under his wing and spends several days explaining his job to him. By the end of the first week, the poor member of staff has met none of his colleagues, neither has he tried his hand at the job he was appointed to do. He's discovered an awful lot about John's job however.

### Trish throws him in at the deep end

Trish introduces her new member of staff to one of his colleagues and asks him to show the newcomer around. After a whirlwind tour of the premises the new member of staff is left to rummage through the contents of the desk left by the previous employee. By lunchtime he is feeling somewhat lost and bewildered. Trish cannot see that there should be any problem. 'He knows the job,' she says 'why doesn't he get on with it!'

### Mark holds a short staff meeting

A week before Mark's new member of staff is due to begin work, Mark holds a brief staff meeting and establishes a schedule of meetings and visits for the newcomer. He asks one member of staff to take overall responsibility for the induction programme and stresses that he wants to see an outline of the proposed programme before the newcomer arrives.

At the end of the first day Mark meets with the new member of staff to make sure all went well and to establish a series of further meetings to ensure that the new employee is supported in his attempts to grasp the job and get up to speed. The meetings, which initially focus upon getting to know the premises, the staff and the customers, gradually develop into discussions about technical aspects of the job and training requirements.

Much sooner than expected Mark is able to tell his new staff member that the induction period is ended and that from now on, their meetings will take the form of regular performance review and appraisal discussions.

## DISCUSSION POINTS

1. Do you have clear goals and targets? What would you describe as success in your company?

2. Do the targets you set for your staff have any relation to the goals you have set for your organisation?

3. Having recruited the right staff, do you have a system in place to help them achieve their goals?

4. Do you regularly meet with your staff to discuss progress and performance?

Appendix:
# Qualifications

Some of the more well known qualifications you may come across include:

## A levels

A level GCEs continue to be the examinations which are traditionally taken at 18 years of age after two years of study in the sixth form at school or at college. Usually candidates sit two or three A Level examinations and the subjects studied are often allied to traditional school subjects. For years A levels have been the young person's key to higher education or 'good' jobs. They are still the hoops through which countless people jump each year.

## Certificate of secondary eduction (CSE)

These school examinations were developed in the mid- to late 1960s to run alongside the better known General Certificate of Education. A grade 1 CSE was considered to be equivalent to an O level GCE.

## Business and technology education council (BTEC)

This organisation provides a wide range of programmes of study related to many occupational fields in England, Wales and Northern Ireland. BTEC courses are run in schools, colleges of further education, universities, companies and training centres. People study for BTEC qualifications in a variety of ways: as full-time students, on day release, through open learning or distance learning packages, or as part-time evening class students.

BTEC qualifications are available in subjects such as: the built environment, business and finance, caring services, computing and information systems, design, distribution, engineering, home economics, horticulture, hotel and catering, information technology, land based industries, leisure services, management, public administration and science.

There are a range of levels at which various subjects can be studied.

- BTEC first Certificate/Diploma
- BTEC GNVQ level 2
- BTEC National Certificate/Diploma
- BTEC GNVQ level 3
- BTEC Higher National Certificate/Diploma
- BTEC Continuing Education Certificate/Diploma and modules

### General Certificate in Education (GCEs)

Otherwise known as 'O' levels, these examinations were usually taken at 16 years of age. They tested knowledge of a fairly traditional range of school subjects and they were seen as the gateway to further education or 'good' jobs. Five 'O' level passes including maths and English were the goal to which school pupils and their parents aspired. GCEs were the 'gold standard' against which other examinations were judged. Few other public examinations have been held in such high esteem by employers. They continue to be highly valued end of school 'basic' qualifications – undeservedly so perhaps.

### General Certificate of Secondary Education (GCSEs)

General Certificates of Secondary Education are the present standard by which many young people are judged at the end of their compulsory school life. They replaced earlier GCE and CSE certificates which came under increasing criticism from many educationalists, who argued that CSEs were undervalued because of the continued existence of the older more traditional GCE 'O' levels. In general a GCSE grade C or above is considered to be equivalent to an 'O' level pass. Four or five GCSE passes at grade C or above can be the key to a wide range of jobs or further education opportunities providing Maths and English are among them.

### General National Vocational Qualifications (GNVQs)

These are new qualifications which offer an alternative route towards higher education or employment. Each GNVQ is designed to test skills and knowledge within a broad area of work. With GCSE and 'A' Levels students tend to study fairly standard school subjects. GNVQ however, offers the possibility of gaining a qualification in something that is more closely related to the world of work. The earliest GNVQs were offered in the fields of Art and Design, Business, Health and Social Care, Leisure and Tourism, and Manufacturing. Further subject areas are now being added all the time. Initially there were two levels of GNVQ on offer. Level 2 is considered to be pitched at about the same standard as four GCSEs and it normally takes a year to complete. Level 3 was designed to be the equivalent of at least two 'A' levels but this is where similarities end.

GNVQs are radically different to most 'A' levels. GNVQs are made up of 'Units', and each unit is made up of a number of 'Elements'. Students attain a GNVQ by showing an assessor that they have gained the necessary skill or knowledge to meet the requirements of each element. At GNVQ level 2, for example, a student would have to demonstrate his ability to use information technology. He would attain this unit by showing that he can:

- set up storage systems;
- input information;
- edit, organise and integrate information from different sources;
- select and use formats for presenting information;
- evaluate features and facilities of given applications;
- deal with errors and faults on computers.

Each of the above is an element adding towards the Information Technology Unit. With GNVQ a student has to collect evidence through project work, demonstration, and study, to show an assessor that he has gained the necessary skill and knowledge.

GNVQ students are able to work at their own pace and at their own level. They are assessed on each element when they think they are ready. There is no formal end of course examination. Each student keeps a record and they can be credited with having achieved each unit. Some may not complete the full range of units necessary for the award of a GNVQ but their achievements will have been recognised and they will be able to continue adding units to their portfolio of achievement through further education should they wish to.

# Glossary

**ACAS**. The Advisory, Conciliation and Arbitration Service (ACAS) plays an important role in advising and supplying information on industrial relations to employers. Its officers also play a conciliatory role in trying to solve trade disputes and complaints made to Industrial Tribunals. They are respected by employers and employees alike.

**Appointment**. The formal process of bringing a person into an organisation.

**Appraisal**. Assessment of an employee's performance and contribution to the goals and targets of an organisation. Appraisal is a means of identifying achievement and solving individual problems in the workplace. Appraisal also enables employers and staff members to identify success as well as areas for development and further training. Appraisal is sometimes seen as part of a larger process of performance review, although some employers draw clear distinctions between the two activities.

**Assessment centre**. A means of testing a candidate's suitability for a job through the use of a variety of tests, work simulations and in-depth interviews. The term 'assessment centre' relates to these activities. It is not a geographical location.

**Casual workers**. Staff employed for short periods – a week or perhaps less.

**Closed questions**. Questions designed to gain simple factual information in an interview. The question 'Do you have a driving licence?' for example requires a simple 'closed' answer 'Yes I do', or 'No I don't.'

**Contract of employment**. A formal statement of the terms and conditions of employment. Some employers prefer to give a simple written statement rather than a contract. Both are legitimate, providing they cover the areas required by the Employment Department publication (PL 700 Rev2), and providing employees receive them within two months of commencing work.

**Employment legislation**. A general term describing the variety of laws or statutes which govern employment matters. See the 'List of Statutes' on page 149.

**Equal opportunities**. A general term embracing a number of laws which prohibit discrimination in the workplace.

**Experience**. An ability to do a job due to learning which has taken place in other job situations. Not all experience is 'good' or 'relevant'.

**Freelance staff**. Many companies requiring a diversity of specific skills for short periods of time, rely on freelance staff who remain essentially self-employed while they undertake specific tasks for an organisation.

**Induction**. The process of 'bringing someone into an organisation', ensuring that they become familiar with the geography, structure, culture and procedures of an organisation to enable them to become effective in their jobs as quickly as possible.

**Interview**. 'Inter' means between. An interview is a discussion between two parties to discover whether they could work together. Where an employer uses a number of interviewers in order to gain a better insight into a candidate, this is sometimes known as a panel interview.

**Job descriptions**. Short statements which describe the essential elements of a job.

**Job title**. A simple phrase which describes the activity or key responsibility of a job. A good job title also seeks to convey an impression of the level of responsibility the job carries within a company.

**National Vocational Qualifications (NVQs)**. These are workplace qualifications which seek to recognise 'competence' in the job rather than academic knowledge. See Appendix 1 for more details.

**Open questions**. Questions designed to encourage a candidate to talk about himself, his interests or his experience. Open questions usually begin with phrases such as 'How do you see . . .?', 'How do you feel about . . .?' 'What do you think of . . .?'

**Person specification**. A short statement describing the ideal person to fulfil the requirements of a given job.

**Performance review**. Usually a one-to-one discussion between an employee and his manager concerning the factors which affect the employee's performance in the workplace. Such discussions are frequently included in a wider process of appraisal.

**Qualifications**. The formal recognition of ability or knowledge. There are a large number of types of and level of qualifications. See Appendix 1.

**Recruitment**. A process of identifying an organisation's need and then meeting that need through the appointment of an apparently skilled, able and well-motivated member of staff.

**References**. Confidential statements about candidates from previous bosses, managers or 'worthy' people in the community who can comment on a candidate's integrity or suitability for a job.

**Responsibilities**. Aspects of a job for which an employee is responsible. Responsibilities tend to have long-term value and are therefore, preferable to 'tasks' when describing a job.

**Selection tests**. A variety of tests which seek to provide objective evidence about a candidate's suitability for a given occupation. Some tests measure personality traits while others test skill and ability through work samples.

**Sequential interviews**. A sequence of mini interviews, each one specifically designed to test a candidate's ability in a different aspect of a given job.

**Shortlisting**. The process of reducing a large number of applicants to a small number of candidates who appear to be appropriately skilled and qualified to fulfil the requirements of the job.

**Skills**. Specific abilities related to a job.

**Tasks**. Short-term jobs which are given to employees.

**Testimonials**. Non-confidential statements about a candidate or his suitability for a job, written by previous employers or others in the community who know him.

# Further Reading

*Body Langauge*, Allan Pease (Sheldon Press, 1992).

*The Communicating Organisation*, Michael Blakstad and Aldwyn Cooper (Institute of Personnel and Development, 1995).

*Effective Employee Communications*, Michael Bland and Peter Jackson (Kogan Page, 1990).

*How to be an Even Better Manager*, Michael Armstrong (Kogan Page, 1988).

*How to Communicate at Work*, Ann Dobson (How To Books, 1994).

*How to Conduct Staff Appraisals*, Nigel Hunt (How To Books, 1994).

*How to Employ and Manage Staff*, Wendy Wyatt (How To Books, 2nd edition, 1995).

*How to Manage People at Work*, John Humphries (How To Books, 1995).

*Improve Your People Skills*, Peter Honey (Institute of Personnel and Development, 1988).

*The Management Handbook*, Arthur Young (Sphere, 1986).

*Not Bosses But Leaders*, John Adair (Kogan Page, 1978).

*Success in Management: Personnel*, Penny Hackett (John Murray, revised 1987).

*Teamwork*, Vincent Nolan (Sphere, 1987).

ACAS (Advisory, Conciliation and Arbitration Service) produce a wide range of helpful, free publications including:
*Employing people: a handbook for small firms*
*Discipline at work*
*Recruitment and Induction*
*Employee communications and consultation*
*The company handbook*
*Employment policies*
*Employee appraisal*
*Effective organisations: the people factor*
*Supervision*
*Recruitment policies for the 1990s*

For details of how to order ACAS Publications please write to: ACAS Reader Ltd, PO Box 404, Leicester LE4 9ZZ; or telephone 0116 246 3346.

**Employment Department Publications**. The following booklets on employment are a selection of the range which can be obtained free of charge from local offices of the Employment Service (Jobcentres).

PL 716 *Individual rights of employees, a guide for employers*
PL 700 (REV2) *Written statement of employment particulars*

# Useful Addresses

Advisory, Conciliation and Arbitration Service (ACAS), 27 Wilton Street, London SW1X 7AZ. Tel: (0171) 210 3600.

Commission for Racial Equality, Elliot House, 10–12 Allington Street, London SW1E 5EH. Tel: (0171) 828 7022.

Department of Education and Employment, Caxton House, Tothill Street, London SW1 9NF. Tel: (0171) 231 4033.

Department of Social Security, Market Towers, 1 Nine Elms Lane, London SW8 5NQ. Tel: (0171) 720 2198. (For leaflets.)

Equal Opportunities Commission, Overseas House, Quay Street, Manchester M3 3HN. Tel: (0161) 833 9244.

Health and Safety Executive, Rose Court, 2 Southwark Bridge, London SE1 9HF. Tel: (0171) 717 6000.

Health and Safety Executive, Magdalen House, Stanley Precinct, Bootle, Merseyside L20 3QZ. Tel: (0151) 951 4000.

# List of Statutes

**Disabled Persons (Employment) Acts 1944, 1958**
Imposes quotas of disabled people which must be employed by medium and large scale companies.
**Employment Act 1989**
Contains provisions against discrimination in employment and training; removes restrictions on the hours of work of young people; limits paid time off for union duties; empowers tribunals to require a deposit for poorly based claims; and miscellaneous other matters.
**Employment Protection Act 1975**
Introduced a wide range of material dealing with employment rights.
**Employment Protection (Consolidation) Act 1978**
Brought together in one statute a very wide range of rules dealing with employment matters. In particular sections 1 to 6 and 11 of the Act concern the right of the individual to receive a written statement of employment particulars.
**Employment Protection (Part-Time Employees) Regulations 1995**
Extended many employment rights to part-time workers.
**Equal Pay Act 1970 (amended 1983)**
Introduced the principle that men and women are generally entitled to equal pay for similar work.
**Factories Act 1961**
Contains a large number of regulations concerning safety in the work place.
**Health and Safety At Work Act 1974**
Provides a code of general principles ar.d an enforcement mechanism for health and safety matters.
**Information For Employees Regulations 1989**
Requires employers to bring certain information regarding health and safety to the attention of their employees.
**Misrepresentation Act 1967**
Enables a person entering into a contract, including a contract of employment, to claims for damages if he suffers damage due to the misrepresentation of terms.

**Race Relations Act 1976**

Sets out the law regarding race discrimination. In effect, no employer, regardless of the number of people he employs, may discriminate on racial grounds.

**Rehabilitation Of Offenders Act 1974**

Allows persons convicted of relatively minor offences, after a period of non-offending, to have their convictions treated as 'spent'. A job applicant is not obliged to admit to a spent conviction, and may not be dismissed or discriminated against on the grounds of that conviction.

**Sex Discrimination Act 1975**

Sets out the law governing sex discrimination. In effect, it is unlawful to discriminate on the grounds of sex in the recruitment of staff, the terms of employment, or in training or promotion. The Act protects men as well as women and therefore notions of 'positive' discrimination are also unlawful. It is also illegal to discriminate on the grounds of marital status.

**Trade Union Reform and Employment Rights Act 1993**

Reforms trade union law, and amends the Employment Protection (Consolidation) Act 1978 to improve employment protection rights, including the right to a written statement of employment particulars.

# Index

## Organising Effective Training
**How to plan and run successful courses and seminars**

James Chalmers

Industry, public services, colleges, community groups, and organisations of all kinds urgently need to train their people in a wide variety of much needed skills. But however knowledgeable the tutors are, if a training event has been badly organised it will be a waste of everyones time and money. This book explains how to plan and organise really successful training events. The method can be applied to anything, from team building to technical courses, and from a one hour briefing up to events lasting several days. The step-by-step approach is easy to follow, and will work equally well with organisers who are unfamiliar with the subject to be trained, as well as professional trainers. If you are ever asked to put on an event, or if you want someone to run one for you, then this will give all the necessary guidance and ensure a successful outcome every time. James Chalmers BSc CEng MIEE has worked in industry for 25 years, and has much experience of running successful training programmes.

*160pp illus. 1 85703 329 9.*

## How to Employ & Manage Staff
**A practical handbook for managers and supervisors**

Wendy Wyatt

Now in a revised second edition, this easy to use handbook is intended for all young managers, supervisors and students whose work will involve them in recruiting and managing staff. Ideal for quick reference, it provides a ready-made framework of modern employment practice from recruitment onwards. It provides a clear account of how to apply the health & safety at work regulations, how to handle record-keeping, staff development, grievance and disciplinary procedures, maternity and sick leave and similar matters for the benefit of the organisation and its employees. The book includes a useful summary of current employment legislation and is complete with a range of model forms, letters, notices and similar documents. Wendy Wyatt MIPD is a Personnel Management and

Employment Consultant; her other books include *Recruiting Success* and *Jobhunt.*

*176pp illus. 1 85703 167 9. 2nd edition.*

## How to Write a Report
### A step-by-step guide to effective report writing

John Bowden

Communicating effectively on paper is an essential skill for today's business or professional person. Written by an experienced manager and staff trainer, this well-presented handbook provides a very clear step-by-step framework for every individual, whether dealing with professional colleagues, customers, clients, suppliers or junior or senior staff. Contents: Preparation and planning. Collecting and handling information. Writing the report: principles and techniques. Improving your thinking. Improving presentation. Achieving a good writing style. Making effective use of English. How to choose and use illustrations. Choosing paper, covers and binding. Appendices (examples, techniques, checklists), glossary, index. 'Most of us have a need to write a report of some kind at various times, and this book has real value . . . Thoroughly commendable.' *IPS Journal.* John Bowden BSc (Econ) MSc has long experience both as a professional manager in industry, and as a Senior Lecturer running courses in accountancy, auditing and effective communication.

*176pp illus. 1 85703 211 X. 3rd edition.*

## How to Prepare a Business Plan
### Laying the right foundations for business success

Matthew Record

A business plan is the most important commercial document you will ever have to produce, whether you are just starting out in business, or are already trading. A well thought out and carefully structured plan will be crucial to the survival and longterm success of the enterprise. It will provide a detailed map of exactly where it is going, and help you forestall any problems long before they arise. A third of all new businesses fail in their first year, and of the rest a staggering 95 per cent will not make it beyond 5 years. Poor planning has been identified as the major cause of business failure. With the odds so stacked against success, make sure YOUR business gets off to the right start. Matthew Record is a business consultant specialising in the preparation of business plans for a variety of commercial clients. His company, Phoenix Business Plans, is based in Dorset.

*158pp illus. 1 85703 178 4.*

## Investing in People
**How to help your organisation achieve higher standards and a competitive edge**

Dr Harley Turnbull

Investors in People is the most important quality programme for change in the 1990s. As Sir Brian Wolfson, Chairman, Investors In People, UK, said (*Employment News*, June 1995), 'Thousands of companies across the country are involved in gaining sustainable, competitive advantage for their business by introducing the winning principles of the Investors in People Standard'. The National Advisors Council for Education and Training Targets has set an Investor in People target for the year 2000: - 70% of all organisations employing 200 or more employees and 35% employing 50 or more, to be recognised as Investors in People. Dr Harley Turnbull, a chartererd Occupational Psychologist and Member of the Institute of Personnel and Development, has professional experience of IIP both as an internal HRD manager and external consultant.

*160pp illus. 1 85703 188 1.*

## How to Master Business English
**Improving your communication skills**

Michael Bennie

Are you communicating effectively? Do your business documents achieve the results you want? Or are they too often ignored or misunderstood? Good communication is the key to success in any business. Whether you are trying to sell a product, answer a query or complaint, or persuade colleagues, the way you express yourself is often as important as what you say. With lots of examples, checklists and questionnaires to help you, the new edition of this book will speed you on your way. 'An excellent book — . . . Altogether most useful for anyone seeking to improve their communication skills.' *IPS Journal.* 'Gives guidance on writing styles for every situation . . . steers the reader through the principles and techniques of effective letter-writing and document-planning.' *First Voice.* 'Useful chapters on grammar, punctuation and spelling. Frequent questionnaires and checklists enable the reader to check progress.' *Focus (Society of Business Teachers).* 'The language and style is easy to follow . . . Excellent value for money.' *Spoken English.*

*208pp illus. 1 85703 129 6. 2nd edition.*

## Winning Presentations
### How to sell your ideas and yourself

Ghassan Hasbani

'Good communication skills' is a phrase repeatedly used in job descriptions and CVs. These skills can make or break people's careers and are highly regarded by employers and organisations. One of the most important skills is the ability to present and put your ideas across whether you are an employee or an independent consultant, a civil servant or businessperson, a school teacher or a university lecturer, a member of the local club or someone starting a career in politics. No matter who you are or what kind of work you do, you always need to communicate with people on different occasions and present to them ideas, news, or achievements. This step-by-step guide tells you all you need to know in order to become confident in giving effective presentations, that will help you succeed in your life and career. Presenting is not necessarily a gift, it is a skill which can be learned or acquired and this book will help you do that. Ghassan Hasbani started writing and presenting for television at the age of 16. He currently works as a telecommunications engineer, where he uses his skills to present new technologies in seminars and lectures. He also works as a visiting university lecturer teaching management and communication skills to undergraduates.

*160pp illus. 1 85703 304 3.*

## How to Manage an Office
### Creating and managing a successful workplace

Ann Dobson

Good office management is one of the keys to success in any organisation. The benefits are a happy and productive staff, satisfied customers, and a sound base from which to tackle such issues as growth and change within the organisation. Written by an experienced office manager and business consultant, this book suggests a complete practical framework for the well run office. It discusses what an office is for, the office as communications, the office as workplace, equipment, hygiene, health and security, external appearances, managing visitors, handling orders and information, managing office supplies, the office budget, staff management, and managing an office move.

*160 pp illus. 1 85703 049 4.*

## How to Write a Press Release
### A step-by-step guide to getting your message across

Peter Bartram

Every day, newspapers and magazines are deluged with thousands of press releases. Which stories make an editor sit and take up notice? Why do some press releases never get used? This book explains all. 'Takes you step-by-step through the process.' *Home Run Magazine.* 'Shows how to style and build a news story that carries value for readers . . . I recommend this book.' *Writers Forum.* 'Yes! Yes, yes, yes! Here at last is a book that tells it like it is.' *Writers Monthly.* 'Compulsory reading.' *Phoenix/AGCAS.* If you have ever had a press release rejected – or want to win 'free' column inches for your organisation – *How to Write a Press Release* is the handbook for you. Peter Bartram BSc(Econ) is one of Britain's most published business writers and journalists, with more than 2,500 feature articles and seven books to his credit. He edits the magazine *Executive Strategy.*

*144pp illus. 1 85703 163 6. 2nd edition.*

# How To Books

How To Books provide practical help on a large range of topics. They are available through all good bookshops or can be ordered direct from the distributors. Just tick the titles you want and complete the form on the following page.

___ Apply to an Industrial Tribunal (£7.99)
___ Applying for a Job (£7.99)
___ Applying for a United States Visa (£15.99)
___ Be a Freelance Journalist (£8.99)
___ Be a Freelance Secretary (£8.99)
___ Be a Local Councillor (£8.99)
___ Be an Effective School Governor (£9.99)
___ Become a Freelance Sales Agent (£9.99)
___ Become an Au Pair (£8.99)
___ Buy & Run a Shop (£8.99)
___ Buy & Run a Small Hotel (£8.99)
___ Cash from your Computer (£9.99)
___ Career Planning for Women (£8.99)
___ Choosing a Nursing Home (£8.99)
___ Claim State Benefits (£9.99)
___ Communicate at Work (£7.99)
___ Conduct Staff Appraisals (£7.99)
___ Conducting Effective Interviews (£8.99)
___ Copyright & Law for Writers (£8.99)
___ Counsel People at Work (£7.99)
___ Creating a Twist in the Tale (£8.99)
___ Creative Writing (£9.99)
___ Critical Thinking for Students (£8.99)
___ Do Voluntary Work Abroad (£8.99)
___ Do Your Own Advertising (£8.99)
___ Do Your Own PR (£8.99)
___ Doing Business Abroad (£9.99)
___ Emigrate (£9.99)
___ Employ & Manage Staff (£8.99)
___ Find Temporary Work Abroad (£8.99)
___ Finding a Job in Canada (£9.99)
___ Finding a Job in Computers (£8.99)
___ Finding a Job in New Zealand (£9.99)
___ Finding a Job with a Future (£8.99)
___ Finding Work Overseas (£9.99)
___ Freelance DJ-ing (£8.99)
___ Get a Job Abroad (£10.99)
___ Get a Job in America (£9.99)
___ Get a Job in Australia (£9.99)
___ Get a Job in Europe (£9.99)
___ Get a Job in France (£9.99)
___ Get a Job in Germany (£9.99)
___ Get a Job in Hotels and Catering (£8.99)
___ Get a Job in Travel & Tourism (£8.99)
___ Get into Films & TV (£8.99)
___ Get into Radio (£8.99)
___ Get That Job (£6.99)
___ Getting your First Job (£8.99)
___ Going to University (£8.99)
___ Helping your Child to Read (£8.99)
___ Investing in People (£8.99)
___ Invest in Stocks & Shares (£8.99)

___ Keep Business Accounts (£7.99)
___ Know Your Rights at Work (£8.99)
___ Know Your Rights: Teachers (£6.99)
___ Live & Work in America (£9.99)
___ Live & Work in Australia (£12.99)
___ Live & Work in Germany (£9.99)
___ Live & Work in Greece (£9.99)
___ Live & Work in Italy (£8.99)
___ Live & Work in New Zealand (£9.99)
___ Live & Work in Portugal (£9.99)
___ Live & Work in Spain (£7.99)
___ Live & Work in the Gulf (£9.99)
___ Living & Working in Britain (£8.99)
___ Living & Working in China (£9.99)
___ Living & Working in Hong Kong (£10.99)
___ Living & Working in Israel (£10.99)
___ Living & Working in Japan (£8.99)
___ Living & Working in Saudi Arabia (£12.99)
___ Living & Working in the Netherlands (£9.99)
___ Lose Weight & Keep Fit (£6.99)
___ Make a Wedding Speech (£7.99)
___ Making a Complaint (£8.99)
___ Manage a Sales Team (£8.99)
___ Manage an Office (£8.99)
___ Manage Computers at Work (£8.99)
___ Manage People at Work (£8.99)
___ Manage Your Career (£8.99)
___ Managing Budgets & Cash Flows (£9.99)
___ Managing Meetings (£8.99)
___ Managing Your Personal Finances (£8.99)
___ Market Yourself (£8.99)
___ Master Book-Keeping (£8.99)
___ Mastering Business English (£8.99)
___ Master GCSE Accounts (£8.99)
___ Master Languages (£8.99)
___ Master Public Speaking (£8.99)
___ Obtaining Visas & Work Permits (£9.99)
___ Organising Effective Training (£9.99)
___ Pass Exams Without Anxiety (£7.99)
___ Pass That Interview (£6.99)
___ Plan a Wedding (£7.99)
___ Prepare a Business Plan (£8.99)
___ Publish a Book (£9.99)
___ Publish a Newsletter (£9.99)
___ Raise Funds & Sponsorship (£7.99)
___ Rent & Buy Property in France (£9.99)
___ Rent & Buy Property in Italy (£9.99)
___ Retire Abroad (£8.99)
___ Return to Work (£7.99)
___ Run a Local Campaign (£6.99)
___ Run a Voluntary Group (£8.99)
___ Sell Your Business (£9.99)

| | |
|---|---|
| ___ Selling into Japan (£14.99) | ___ Use the Internet (£9.99) |
| ___ Setting up Home in Florida (£9.99) | ___ Winning Consumer Competitions (£8.99) |
| ___ Spend a Year Abroad (£8.99) | ___ Winning Presentations (£8.99) |
| ___ Start a Business from Home (£7.99) | ___ Work from Home (£8.99) |
| ___ Start a New Career (£6.99) | ___ Work in an Office (£7.99) |
| ___ Starting to Manage (£8.99) | ___ Work in Retail (£8.99) |
| ___ Starting to Write (£8.99) | ___ Work with Dogs (£8.99) |
| ___ Start Word Processing (£8.99) | ___ Working Abroad (£14.99) |
| ___ Start Your Own Business (£8.99) | ___ Working as a Holiday Rep (£9.99) |
| ___ Study Abroad (£8.99) | ___ Working in Japan (£10.99) |
| ___ Study & Learn (£7.99) | ___ Working in Photography (£8.99) |
| ___ Study & Live in Britain (£7.99) | ___ Working in the Gulf (£10.99) |
| ___ Studying at University (£8.99) | ___ Working on Contract Worldwide (£9.99) |
| ___ Studying for a Degree (£8.99) | ___ Working on Cruise Ships (£9.99) |
| ___ Successful Grandparenting (£8.99) | ___ Write a CV that Works (£7.99) |
| ___ Successful Mail Order Marketing (£9.99) | ___ Write a Press Release (£9.99) |
| ___ Successful Single Parenting (£8.99) | ___ Write a Report (£8.99) |
| ___ Survive at College (£4.99) | ___ Write an Assignment (£8.99) |
| ___ Survive Divorce (£8.99) | ___ Write an Essay (£7.99) |
| ___ Surviving Redundancy (£8.99) | ___ Write & Sell Computer Software (£9.99) |
| ___ Take Care of Your Heart (£5.99) | ___ Write Business Letters (£8.99) |
| ___ Taking in Students (£8.99) | ___ Write for Publication (£8.99) |
| ___ Taking on Staff (£8.99) | ___ Write for Television (£8.99) |
| ___ Taking Your A-Levels (£8.99) | ___ Write Your Dissertation (£8.99) |
| ___ Teach Abroad (£8.99) | ___ Writing a Non Fiction Book (£8.99) |
| ___ Teach Adults (£8.99) | ___ Writing & Selling a Novel (£8.99) |
| ___ Teaching Someone to Drive (£8.99) | ___ Writing & Selling Short Stories (£8.99) |
| ___ Travel Round the World (£8.99) | ___ Writing Reviews (£8.99) |
| ___ Use a Library (£6.99) | ___ Your Own Business in Europe (£12.99) |

To: Plymbridge Distributors Ltd, Plymbridge House, Estover Road, Plymouth PL6 7PZ. Customer Services Tel: (01752) 202301. Fax: (01752) 202331.

Please send me copies of the titles I have indicated. Please add postage & packing (UK £1, Europe including Eire, £2, World £3 airmail).

☐ I enclose cheque/PO payable to Plymbridge Distributors Ltd for £ [        ]

☐ Please charge to my ☐ MasterCard, ☐ Visa, ☐AMEX card.

Account No. [                            ]

Card Expiry Date [    ] 19 ☏ **Credit Card orders may be faxed or phoned.**

Customer Name (CAPITALS) ........................................................

Address ............................................................................

........................................................ Postcode ...............

Telephone ........................... Signature ...................................

Every effort will be made to despatch your copy as soon as possible but to avoid possible disappointment please allow up to 21 days for despatch time (42 days if overseas). Prices and availability are subject to change without notice.

BPA